ROTHERHAM & DISTRICT TRANSPORT

VOLUME THREE
By Charles C. Hall, FCIT

Foreword

The author is deeply grateful for all the friends who have made these volumes possible; to Alan Oxer whose help and encouragement - and his hours of work typing out my often nearly illegible manuscripts - has brought this work to its conclusion. I mention with gratitude the help which the late Mr Horace Clayton provided, always being happy to loan photographs from his wonderful lifetime's collection. Again to Paul Fox who has provided numerous illustrations - and helpful discussions over the years of effort - to Pat and Tom who hold a special place - and first read through the original manuscript. The list could go on for pages. David Dodd; Roy Marshall; Mike Fowler; A. B. Cross; C. Carter; David Packer; Roy Brooks and the always helpful staff of the Rotherham Archives Section. To end - if I have inadvertently omitted to mention anyone - please accept my apologies and know that you have my deepest thanks.

Rotherwood
Press

Published by the Rotherwood Press,
the publishing imprint of the
Library and Information Services
Rotherham Central Library
Walker Place
Rotherham, S65 1JH
1999
ISBN 0 903666 93 6

Rotherham

ROTHERHAM & DISTRICT TRANSPORT

CHAPTER 1

War Time

When war was declared in September 1939 there was no feeling that our lads would be back by Christmas. On the contrary, it was thought that the urban population would be annihilated with indiscriminate bombing, and "bomb proof" shelters were already being built in the months before war was declared.

College Square, not long before the start of the second world war. A Sheffield tram waits for its time to leave while a 1935 Bristol-Roe passes. No 85 of the same pattern but dating from 1931 stands while passengers board. *Copyright H B Priestley*

5884

SHEFFIELD CORPORATION, L.M.S. & L.N.E. RAILWAYS
JOINT OMNIBUS COMMITTEE

NATIONAL EMERGENCY

Route
77
SHEFFIELD - ROTHERHAM
DONCASTER

ON AND AFTER SATURDAY, 16th
SEPTEMBER, 1939, THE ABOVE
SERVICE WILL BE SUSPENDED

H. WATSON,
Secretary

Division Street,
Sheffield,
September, 1939

With the outbreak of war notices were issued detailing service cuts. Initially the Sheffield-Rotherham-Doncaster route closed completely.

Apart from this, it was felt that it would be a long war and at once preparations were being made to cover, hopefully, every eventuality. The most serious disadvantage in the the first weeks of the war was the night time blackout. Mr Sykes, the Rotherham Transport Manager, wrote a letter in the local press praising his road staff for the way they were coping. To date there had been two accidents with cars running into the back of buses, while boarding and alighting accidents were increasing. The bus windows were painted blue while the interior lights were shaded - and the head lights were so reduced as to be useless.

The following winter of the "phoney war" was something of an anticlimax as the civilian population adjusted to the black out and plenty of work for all after the between war years of unemployment.

To begin with it was agreed nationally that buses already in the pipeline should be built and generally orders were completed to specification. Rotherham Corporation started the war with a modern fleet consisting of a dozen tramcars, eleven of which were the single end double deckers, new in 1934/35. Additionally, one of the old Rotherham 6 side window un-vestibuled cars, now numbered 12, was still in stock. The bus fleet of some 80 single deck buses, all on Bristol chassis was well maintained and of a comparatively low average age. Finally the trolley bus fleet was varied. Most of the Ransomes, dating from 1931, were still in use as were the four 1928/29 six wheeled Guys. The high powered Guy and AEC six wheelers were "nearly new".

The Mexborough & Swinton trolley bus fleet was unchanged since the arrival of the second hand English Electric buses. The Garretts were frankly beginning to look a little bit dated, though they had proved an excellent purchase and the company was prosperous. The small bus fleet tended to be made up of second hand vehicles, with a tendency to come from the Yorkshire Traction Co Ltd at Barnsley. The Mexborough company had been connected with Yorkshire Traction since 1931 when the British Electric Traction Company had purchased most of the National Electric Construction Co.'s shares which included the Mexborough & Swinton capital.

With the war in progress, an order was placed during October 1939 for eight trolley bus chassis from yet another newcomer to Rotherham, Sunbeam Commercial vehicles, the bodies once more to be built by East Lancashire Coachbuilders. The six wheel chassis were to a new design by Sunbeam, the prototype of which was prepared for the 1939 Commercial Motor Show - which because of the war never took place. The MS.2 chassis was designed for use under a double deck body, with B.T.H. equipment. The GEC WT268E motor, which was fitted to the off side of the chassis close to the front rear axle, was compound wound to give limited regeneration, and developed 107 HP at 525 volts on the one hour rating. The 12 volt dynamo for lighting was driven directly from the front end of the motor. The body seated 40 passengers and was made similar to those previously supplied. The original fleet numbers were 70 to 77. Bus No 70 had its acceptance tests at Rotherham on 27 October 1940. The laden weight was 11 tons 1 cwt and 2 qtrs.; 36 seconds was required from standing start to 20 mph whilst the maximum speed ascending Whinney Hill was 22 mph - also from stand. The time taken over the whole 14 miles of the route, with 6 stops per mile, was 58 minutes. The Rotherham specifications asked for an acceleration from standing start to 30 mph in 14 seconds - with its East Lancashire 40 seat body fully laden - and a top speed of not less than 40 mph. Much was made of "the exceptionally robust main chassis frame in high tensile steel, which was eleven inches deep on the most heavily loaded sections, with 3½ inch wide flanges. The remainder of the batch entered service during November and December 1940. In a report to his Committee in February 1941, the Manager reported that all eight were delivered at a 10% cost increase. Already a further eight had been ordered in April 1940 "subject to Ministry consents" and these, numbers 82 to 89, entered service in December 1942. At 21 March 1943, the trolley bus fleet total had risen to its maximum of 75 vehicles.

From the outbreak of war, services were reduced as much as possible to limit the demand for petrol and diesel oil. By October only 71% of the pre-war services were being provided. The long distances routes to Worksop and Harworth were closed down. These routes had provided some of the Ravenfield and Braithwell requirements and arrangements were made to continue services to those places. The Sheffield and Maltby joint service was curtailed from 16 September 1939 to operate only as far as the Whiston Cross-roads. There were strong complaints from the users of the service. The traffic over the truncated route was very heavy and the Rotherham single deck buses were being greatly over loaded. An inspector's report of 15 August 1940 noted that Rotherham bus No 108 was conveying 52 passengers on

the journey from Whiston. This compared with Sheffield providing its largest 6 wheel double deck Leyland Titanic's on the route. There was a note of Sheffield No 109 operating from Whiston on 13 September 1940 being barely sufficient for the passenger demand.

One of the Sheffield Leyland Titanics in wartime grey livery, not on a Rotherham Route but of the same type as No 109.

In November 1939, Wickersley Parish Council asked for extra trolley buses from 5.30 am to 6.00 am and complained bitterly of the termination of the Sheffield/Maltby route which they considered should at least be run as far as the Brecks to meet the Rotherham to Maltby service. Maltby Council followed, complaining that now that the Sheffield route was closed, the trolley buses were overloaded and they wanted extra buses between 6.15 and 6.33 am. In September 1940, a meeting had already been arranged by the Regional Transport Commission with the Sheffield manager, Mr Watson and Mr Sykes at the head office. At Sheffield a proposed timetable for a reinstatement of the through service to Maltby had been produced - Mr Sykes was definitely against the proposal - in his opinion there was no justifiable demand for the service.

A year previously the Ministry had agreed to the installation of trolley bus wiring from Westgate to the Rotherham boundary at Templeborough. This was installed at once and in January 1940 a timetable service from Maltby to Templeborough via Rotherham was provided.

At the December Rotherham Council meeting it was agreed that through trolley buses should be run from Kimberworth and Dalton to Templeborough. These services, presumably at peak periods, were never detailed in the timetable. In Mr Sykes' opinion, the additions were sufficient for the Maltby and Wickersley residents even if they had to change at Templeborough on to a tram for Sheffield. After the enquiry, the Regional

ROTHERHAM CORPORATION   TRANSPORT DEPARTMENT

TROLLEY BUS SERVICES—TEMPLEBORO'

Commencing Monday, March 18th, a Workmen's Service of Trolley Buses will operate
from various outside termini to Templeboro' direct as under:

MONDAY to FRIDAY.

From Wickersley	From Worry Goose Lane	From Thrybergh	From Greasbro'	From Rawmarsh, Kilnhurst Rd.
5 25 a.m.	5 30 a.m.	5 25 a.m.	5 28 a.m.	5 20 a.m.
7 25 "	7 30 "	7 22 "	7 20 "	7 20 "
1 25 p.m.	1 30 p.m.	1 25 p.m.	1 28 p.m.	1 20 p.m.
9 25 "	9 30 "	9 25 "	9 25 "	9 20 "

SATURDAY.

5 25 a.m.	5 30 a.m.	5 25 a.m.	5 28 a.m.	5 20 a.m.
7 25 "	7 30 "	7 22 "	7 20 "	7 20 "

MONDAY to FRIDAY.

To Wickersley	To Worry Goose Lane	To Thrybergh	To Greasbro'	To Rawmarsh, Kilnhurst Rd.
6 5 a.m.	6 7 a.m.	6 4 a.m.	6 6 a.m.	6 10 a.m.
2 5 p.m.	2 7 p.m.	2 4 p.m.	2 6 p.m.	2 10 p.m.
5 5 "	5 7 "	5 3 "	5 6 "	5 10 "
10 5 "	10 7 "	10 4 "	10 6 "	10 10 "

SATURDAY.

6 5 a.m.	6 7 a.m.	6 4 a.m.	6 6 a.m.	6 10 a.m.
12 5 p.m.	12 7 p.m.	12 4 p.m.	12 6 p.m.	12 10 p.m.

When the trolley bus extension to Templeborough was opened, the peak hour services from all sides of Rotherham never appeared in the timetable. However when the route opened a notice detailing these services was displayed on the bus windows

Commissioners decided that the Sheffield timetable should be implemented and the through service from Sheffield to Maltby be reintroduced from 7 October 1940. It is not known why the shortened service did not run from Whiston Cross Roads as far as the Brecks on the trolley bus route. It would seem to have been designed to prevent passengers from Maltby using the normal route to Sheffield.

Having settled the dispute, somewhat arbitrarily, on the Sheffield and Maltby route, attention turned to the Rotherham and Sheffield tramway, with trolley buses now running to Templeborough. During the early winter of 1940, the joint tram service tended to be very irregular during the early morning period with numerous letters of complaint to the local press. For example, on 21 January 1940, Rotherham car No 10 - due in Sheffield at 1.20,

The timetable for service 23 - Maltby to Templeborough. One bus maintained the service at an hour and a half interval.

Route No—23.

MALTBY TEMPLEBOROUGH

	n a.m	n	n	n p.m										
Maltby ...		7 45	9 15	10 45	12 15	1 45	3 15	4 45	6 15	7 45	9 15	10 45		
Rotherham High Street ...		8 15	9 45	11 15	12 45	2 15	3 45	5 15	6 45	8 15	9 45	11 15		
Templeborough ...		8 33	10 3	11 33	1 3	2 33	4 3	5 33	7 3	8 33	10 3			
Rotherham All Saints Square	7 15	8 45	10 15	11 45	1 15	2 45	4 15	5 45	7 15	8 45	10 15			
Maltby ...	7 45	9 15	10 45	12 15	1 45	3 15	4 45	6 15	7 45	9 15	10 45			

Intermediate passengers may travel by this through Service.

On journeys to Templeborough the terminus in Rotherham is the bottom of Wellgate and on journeys to Maltby, the starting point in Rotherham is All Saints Square.

turned back at Temple Street with a frozen air-brake - the driver refusing to go forward using the electric brake. On the same day the crossover points were frozen at the Bessemer Gates and the 1.15 p.m. trip from there to Intake was delayed for 15 minutes, while Rotherham No 8 ran into Sheffield No 163 at the Bawtry Road stop. The day before Rotherham No 3 had jumped the automatic points at Newhall Road fouling both tracks. Two days later the Sheffield car No 23 on its journey to Sheffield was held up by a Rotherham car, again No 3, at Temple Street, when the points jammed and the Rotherham car finally went forward to Tinsley depot where the car was turned.

Templeborough terminus with one of the Ransome/Craven trolley buses waiting "its time" before travelling to Bramley (Route 22), a part way stage on the Maltby route. Courtesy Roy Brook.

It was admitted there had been gaps of up to 30 minutes without a car. Mr Sykes finally sent a letter of protest to Mr Watson in December 1940. He wrote "Complaints are continually being published regarding the service and Rotherham seems to be the scapegoat for the trouble. I propose to bring the matter up before my Committee and very strongly suggest that the service shall be split at Templeborough and passengers from Sheffield change here". Mr Watson replied at once, pouring oil on troubled waters suggesting they should meet to discuss the trouble. Although the complaint had been made to Sheffield by Mr Sykes, his own town councillors continued to complain about their service to Templeborough. At the December 1940 meeting, in response to questions, the Transport Department chairman referred to the congestion in All Saints Square between 7.30 and 9.30 am. It had been suggested that through buses from the Housing Scheme could be run through to Templeborough avoiding the transfer to the trams. It was noted that trolley buses had been standing idle at the time in Howard Street waiting to take people to Templeborough - but they seemed to prefer the trams. The through running of the trolley buses from outside areas to Templeborough had already been tried and proved a failure. In January 1941 it was admitted that only 4 trams were available for the Templeborough peak service and it was not understood why the trolley vehicles were not used "to the fullest extent". It was then admitted that for the first two months of trolley vehicle operation to Templeborough, the vehicles "did not earn their keep". Strangely at this period the operation of the through buses had not been advertised - while the usual timetables were now "not available".

On 25 May 1940, the department inserted an advertisement in the local press asking for applications for the post of temporary women conductors at a wage of £2.18.6d per week; only single ladies of a height not less than 5 ft 5 ins aged between 21 and "under 30" of a "superior education" need apply. Married women need not apply, while it would be an advantage if the applicant lived "within walking distance" of the Rawmarsh Road Depot. The first applicants were receiving training by the end of June. In August the upper age limit was raised to 35 whilst married women might be taken on - each case to be decided on its merits - and no women whose husband was already employed would be considered.

In April 1940, J Mellor, the proprietor of the colliery bus service from High Green by way of Thorpe to New Stubbin and Rawmarsh colliery was brought before the court to answer a charge of not operating the service on the morning of January 12th. The case was conflicting - he was supposed to leave High Green at 5.40 am - but on that morning all the colliers had already been picked up by a lorry sent from the colliery. Apparently his authorised time was too late for the colliers' starting time - and the colliery management put on the lorry. Mellor said that it was no good following with no passengers, particularly with the wartime fuel restrictions, and in any case he was thinking of giving up the service - which he did. The Regional Transport Commissioners decided the service was needed and Rotherham Corporation was told to take it over. There was a reference to Mellor's vehicle on his colliery service in November 1934, when a Sheffield inspector at the Black Bull Inn near Thorpe Hesley saw a red canvas covered lorry registration No AWA 289 which passed him with a seated load of passengers coming from the Rotherham direction.

A new Royal Ordnance factory was built to the east of the Maltby terminus on the road to Tickhill and the extra traffic caused deep troubles for the Rotherham management. In May 1941, Mr Sykes proposed that the Maltby trolley bus route should be extended to the "boundary of the permitted area" but his committee decided not to proceed with extension. Meanwhile Sheffield Corporation, using its double deck buses was running through to the Royal Ordnance factory as required. By October 1941 Mr Sykes wrote to Mr Watson pointing out that on the Sheffield - Maltby and Sheffield - Royal Ordnance factory routes, Sheffield was operating 420 miles a week excess mileage over the agreed equal division of mileage and receipts. Rotherham already owed 17,000 excess miles. It had been suggested that, rather than having to run single deck duplicates, Rotherham should obtain some double deck buses, but Mr Sykes considered that at the time it was not possible to obtain double deck vehicles. It would seem that his centre exit single deck bus policy was finally in doubt, nevertheless it is thought that no application was made to the Ministry at the time as to the possibility of Rotherham being supplied with any "utility" double deck buses which were being built. There were many extra services needed to the factory from all parts of the area, and the Sheffield/Maltby route came into its share. From Monday 26 January 1942 Rotherham commenced running buses three times a day from Canklow to the Royal Ordnance factory. This was to be included into the Sheffield/Maltby pool "in a similar manner to the Sheffield Royal Ordnance factory buses". Rotherham added an additional "peak" service from Brinsworth Road, Canklow to

Sheffield in May 1942, the receipts from this being added to the pool "as a war time measure only". From 8 February 1943 to cover part of Rotherham's share in the route, it was agreed that on the service "for the conveyance of workmen to the factory" Rotherham would operate the service "entirely". Three Rotherham buses were parked overnight at Sheffield Leadmill Road garage to cover this requirement, where they were cleaned by Sheffield staff. The arrangement lasted for a year until May 1944 when, due to changes in working hours at the factory, these arrangements became unnecessary.

One of the small proprietors who provided transport to the Royal Ordnance Factory near Maltby was Billies Coaches of Mexborough. He provided a regular service from Mexborough to and from the factory for workpeople. Probably used at that time would be ET 9561 with a Cravens body dating from 1936.

The first winter of the war was the severest for many years - and the Rotherham fleet suffered exceedingly. In February it was noted that after the severe weather one out of every three buses were under repair for broken springs and other damage - the buses had been involved in 52 collisions. For a period reduced services were provided, until sufficient buses were available. In the issue of the Rotherham Advertiser for February 10 1940 was a "Public Notice". Rotherham Corporation Transport Department. Notice is hereby given that owing to shortage of staff and bad road conditions the services on some routes may have to be curtailed. Regular running times cannot be adhered to. Every effort is being made to resume normal services as soon as possible. On the previous Monday, the tram service to Templeborough was abandoned, although Sheffield cars continued to get through to their Templeborough terminus. In some cases services were not resumed for 8 days.

Nine Bristols (L5G) with East Lancashire 32 centre exit bodies had been ordered in September 1939 and these, numbered 157 to 165 (CET 440/448) were delivered in

June 1940. In April 1940, subject to Ministry consent a further nine to the same specification had been ordered. In fact only four Nos. 100 -103 (CET 561/4) were built. They entered service in December 1942 and during the following January, the last new buses in Rotherham until after the war ended. However, the Rotherham management had very early in the war decided on a regular fleet maintenance programme to cover the future years. In December 1941 it was agreed to completely overhaul the chassis and equipment of a bus and trolley bus each month, with the vehicle then going to the East Lancashire Coachworks for a body overhaul. To cover the labour needed, it was agreed to take on extra fitters and two more semi-skilled workers. The cost of each overhaul was estimated at some £500.

Sheffield tram No 217 in collision with a lorry during 1940 near to Templeborough in the Rotherham territory on its way to Sheffield. Only the rear view of the policeman carrying his tin hat shows that it is wartime. The trolley bus wiring is in the picture.

Rotherham was fortunate on the night of the Sheffield blitz in December 1940. Only one Rotherham vehicle, believed to have been tram No 8, suffered damage. This does not seem to have been severe since it was not mentioned in any report and was probably soon returned to service. After the first night of the Blitz there were no tram services in Sheffield next day, Friday 13 December .

Rotherham car No 8 standing at the Rotherham terminus in May 1941. If it was the Rotherham car damaged in the Sheffield blitz, it was soon repaired. Sheffield No 181, just showing, was still not repaired. *Courtesy of D Packer*

Rotherham car No 7 passes under the railway bridge, just past the Washford Bridge crossover used by cars from Rotherham for the first days of service after the Sheffield "blitz".

A Sheffield tram about to "dive" under Ickles railway bridge on its way to Rotherham. From this angle it would not seem possible for there to be sufficient headroom.

It is not known if the Rotherham cars ran to Templeborough on that day but on Saturday cars were run from Rotherham to Washford Bridge in Sheffield - did Sheffield loan cars to Rotherham to cover for difficulties with operating the single end cars in reverse?

However, the return of the bombers on Sunday night (15 December) caused the Rotherham service to be closed again until the following Friday when cars again ran from

A Rotherham tram on its way to Templeborough "fits" under the bridge - the track was interlaced and cars passed under the arch centre. This photo dates from November 1949. The near front corner would never be repaired. *Photo courtesy R J S Wiseman*

Rotherham as far as Norfolk Bridge. Things returned to normal on the Sheffield to Rotherham route when cars again reached Exchange Street on Monday 23 December. However, in spite of Sheffield's loss of 14 cars, in January 1941 the city was loaning cars to Rotherham. Sheffield car No 163 "operated by Rotherham" was mentioned on 8 January and No 183 on 14 February likewise. There was considerable trouble at the Bessemer Gates tramway crossover when "swinging" trolleys at this point where there was no automatic trolley reverser. With the trolley bus wiring installed there were now six wires here and in the "blackout" without any lighting it proved very difficult to find the wire for the return journey. It was quite possible to get the trolley wheel on to the positive trolley bus wire, apart from the trouble of finding the tramway wire. Of particular trouble was a tram at the 10.00 p.m. wartime peak which ran from Bessemer to Intake. There was so much difficulty in the black darkness in finding the right wire that the drivers began to take the car through to Rotherham, time could be kept by leaving the Tinsley depot a little early. However, at Rotherham conductors would not pick up passengers as their trip commenced at Bessemer. This was more involved since at 10.00 p.m. another car left Rotherham for Intake. After some fairly acrimonious correspondence on the subject, both cars were scheduled to run from Rotherham, causing the complaint that longer distance passengers could not get the car because it was filled by shorter stage passengers.

Rotherham was still short of tram cars and the situation caused serious disruptions. An inspector's report for 24 July 1942 noted that "the 5.5. p.m. from Rotherham special "was again out of service, no tramcar available". The trip had been covered as far as Temple Street - the Rotherham "Templeborough" terminus, with a trolley bus. In February 1942, Hadfield's Welfare Officer wrote to

Sheffield asking if instead of turning at the Sheffield Templeborough terminus - some distance up the hill from the Rotherham one - Sheffield would run their cars to Temple Street reverser to meet the trolley buses which Rotherham had already agreed "to do their best" to put on from Rotherham to meet the cars. It is not thought that Sheffield agreed. In any case, the reverser wiring and point operation would not have allowed the reversal without some alteration.

Rotherham car No 12 with its saloon vestibuled in 1939.

The same car in 1942 with top deck vestibules added.

The difficulty in tracing the details of Rotherham tram history was shown just before No 12 was scrapped. The internal tram numbers were erased one by one over each other with the following "discovery". Upper deck 12 – 15 – 31 and saloon 12 – 10 – 15. None of these could have been the original car numbers since No 31 was the "Water car" and No 15 one of the original single deck cars.

Two views of the Templeborough terminus in September 1943 showing the overhead construction for the trolley bus turning circle and the overhead of the tramway reversing triangle.

In February 1942 it was agreed that the motors of cars 1-6 were to be renewed at a cost of £110 per motor. At the November meeting of the Rotherham Council, a councillor suggested that it would help standing passengers and conductors if the first four double seats in the car saloon should be replaced by single seats. After one car had been altered to this arrangement successfully all of them had the modification at a cost of £40 per car. Car No 12, the last of the "old" cars, was fitted with saloon vestibules at an early stage in the war, while it had a further refurbishment later with the addition of top deck vestibules. In January 1943, a surplus Leeds Corporation car, No 125A, was taken on loan at a charge of £25 for the duration of the war. As received, it had saloon vestibules with open end top deck.

Before the saloon vestibules were fitted No 12 was just like No 7 shown here in Sheffield at the Exchange Street terminus in the early 1930s.

At Rotherham it was modified and entered service, as No 14, with vestibules fitted to the top deck. Rotherham was still short of cars and Sheffield helped out when possible.

Leeds No 125A was one of a batch of ten cars, numbered 115 to 126 that were built in 1909. The illustrations are of two cars from the same batch in the same condition of 125A when it reached Rotherham, probably in December 1942. It had not been in service in Leeds since 1939. *Photo Courtesy Keith Terry*

Tram No 14, on loan from Leeds Corporation, as modernised at Rotherham with the top deck ends vestibuled.

Rotherham Car No 14 (Ex Leeds) travelling from the depot to pick up passengers for Ickles in College Square. Ickles was named in Sheffield as "Bessemer Gates". The only thing remaining in the view today is the clock, everything else has been demolished.

In August 1943, the Saturday specials from Rotherham, not normally noted, were operated by Sheffield instead of Rotherham. These consisted of three trips from Rotherham to Tinsley and two more as far as Attercliffe. There is the interesting query about these Attercliffe specials which Rotherham normally operated. They had only two "double ended" cars, No 12 and Ex Leeds No 14 which could operate these duties without trouble. But what happened if they were not available? Did one of the single end cars travel all the way in reverse, or possibly reverse through Tinsley depot on the return from Attercliffe? Neither would have been satisfactory if carrying passengers in reverse. The same question arises

in respect of the football special cars through to Bramall Lane and Owlerton. The only way to serve Bramall Lane without reverse in one direction would have been to go forward from the ground to Woodseats, Abbey Lane and Millhouses to return to Bramall Lane down Wolsey Road. Similarly to Owlerton, cars could have travelled from Bridge Street along the Hillsborough route to Parkside Road and returned from Owlerton by way of Penistone Road - though the curve at the top of Parkside Road was notoriously "tight" to negotiate. However, no one now seems to know how any of these specials were operated.

Trolley bus wiring for one way operation had been installed from the bridge over the River Don near to the

A post war Rotherham trolley bus on the curve out of Rawmarsh Road, under the wiring installed in the early days of the war. *Photo courtesy Rob Mack*

depot continuing along Rawmarsh Road to Chantry Bridge where the wires joined those down Corporation Street. Traffic at the Davy's Corner entrance into All Saint's Square, with the addition of trolley buses from Maltby turning here, was now causing congestion. To relieve this, the trolley buses from Rawmarsh used the Rawmarsh Road entry into Rotherham, going from Frederick Street up Bridgegate turning on an island in All Saint's Square at the top of Bridgegate. The Transport Committee agreed to the alteration on 27 April 1942. Trolley buses for Rawmarsh turned back down Bridgegate and then along Frederick Street to the usual route at Effingham Square. It was noted that this would reduce the peak traffic through the Square by 26 buses an hour. As the war progressed long distance passenger transport became arduous and was frowned upon. One well remembered national advertisement gave the query "Is your journey really necessary?". In 1942 the Ministry of War Transport, in spite of the fuel restrictions, allowed a few of the pre-war shorter coach excursions during the summer. At Rotherham, Riley was allowed to provide country tours on Tuesday evenings and Saturday afternoons, whilst Smart of Greasbrough also ran coaches into Derbyshire. These were closed down in September with final excursions by both operators on Monday September 14th.

During the August holiday week the tram track up High Street was completely re-laid – the first renewal of the lines since 1925. For the week ending August 29 the tram terminus was in Wellgate by Main Street. Trams could reach this point from the depot by travelling up Corporation Street but, having reached Wellgate, how did the single end cars reverse? There seems to be no

information surviving, but as a query – did Sheffield provide the Rotherham part of the service for the week?

By the Autumn of 1942 the effects of the war shortages became acute and further pruning of the services followed. However at the beginning of October, the manager considered that no more evening cuts in services were likely. By the month end he was proved completely wrong with the Ministry imposing the most stringent service curtailments of the war period at the beginning of November. Only workers were allowed to travel after 9

> ### ROTHERHAM CORPORATION TRANSPORT DEPARTMENT.
> # Holidays-at-Home.
> ## *ROCHE ABBEY*
> EACH MONDAY, TUESDAY, WEDNES-DAY, THURSDAY and FRIDAY up to and including the 21st AUGUST, a shuttle service will be operated from 2.30 to 8.00 p.m., between the MALTBY TROLLEY 'BUS TERMINUS and the ENTRANCE TO ROCHE ABBEY GROUNDS.
>
> The service will not operate if the weather is wet.
>
> Fare—Adult, 2d. (single); children under. 14, 1d.
>
> Passengers are advised to take their own food with them, as well as tea and sugar. Hot water for tea, and mineral waters will be provided at reasonable charges, at the Custodian's house in the Abbey grounds; but passengers must take all the necessary crockery with them.
>
> All services running into the country will be augmented, as far as possible, during the period TUESDAY, 28th JULY, 1942, to SUNDAY, 23rd AUGUST, 1942.
>
> T. P. SYKES, M. Inst. T., General Manager.
> 'Rc1'

War time and "Holidays at Home" were the "in thing" with many extra local outdoor events provided for the weekend holiday period. Rotherham Transport provided the facility for a day out at Roche Abbey.

p.m. whilst Sunday services were reduced by 59%. There was a formal meeting of the Council in September to request the Ministry for an extension of 3 years of the 1937 Rotherham Corporation Act which was about to expire. The Transport Chairman explained that they needed to retain the powers in case fuel restrictions became so great that they would have to convert the bus routes to trolley vehicle operation and use electricity.

The Ministry's restriction to buses only carrying workers after 9 p.m. was the subject of bitter resentment. It was felt that at least servicemen on leave should be allowed to travel at any time, whilst evening students were having to walk out of the classes in the middle of lectures in order to catch the last buses before 9 o'clock. A further irritant was the sight, to people having to walk home, of half empty buses passing them. After some correspondence the Regional Commissioners agreed that students should be issued with passes to allow them to travel after nine o'clock whilst forces personnel could also travel – provided that they could prove they were on leave.

The terminus for tram passengers in Rotherham was an island in the middle of the road. In 1942 this was provided with a dark corrugated iron shelter which also tended to keep the passengers "in line". This photograph, showing the shelter was taken in April 1948, not long before the last Sheffield trams were seen in Rotherham.
Courtesy R J S Wiseman

ROTHERHAM CORPORATION TRANSPORT DEPT.

CURTAILMENT OF SERVICES ON AND AFTER 3rd NOVEMBER, 1942.

By Order of the Ministry of War Transport.

'Buses & Trolley 'Buses Only

IT SHOULD BE UNDERSTOOD THAT SUFFICIENT SERVICES WILL BE MAINTAINED AT ALL TIMES TO COVER THE NEEDS OF WORKERS AND CIVIL DEFENCE PERSONNEL.

AFTER 9 P.M. no passenger will be allowed to board vehicles who cannot show a works button, works pass or a permit issued by the Transport Department.

(NOTE.—To deal with employees in small numbers, permit tickets will be issued by the Transport Department to the employer on written application to the Transport Department).

All services will finish at 9 p.m. from the town termini, except tramcars.

All services will commence at 1 p.m. on Sundays and services will be reduced in frequency.

Ordinary passenger services will cease on both types of vehicles after 9 p.m., but passengers will be accepted along the route on both the outward and inward journeys of the 9 p.m. vehicles.

No prepaid tickets or return tickets will be accepted from ordinary passengers after 9 p.m. The following exceptions will be allowed:—

Members of the N.F.S. in uniform,
Members of the Police in uniform,
Members of the Home Guard in uniform, who can exhibit permits.

No members of H.M. Forces allowed to travel after 9 p.m. unless coming home or going back from leave. Such persons will be allowed to ride on production of their travelling warrant or leave pass.

Transport Department,   T. P. SYKES, M.Inst.T.,
    Municipal Buildings,   General Manager,
Rotherham.

The war at sea was causing the loss of ships carrying fuel to Britain and supplies were dangerously low. With hindsight the Ministry could have acted sooner. Trolley buses were included because rubber for tyres was also in short supply, only the trams did not need imported material.

There was new trouble with the uniform staff after a general request for a wage increase had gone to arbitration and, after some delay, had been refused out of hand – to the surprise of the Rotherham chairman and manager. At Sheffield the men went on strike at the end of April – but for the moment their Rotherham colleagues stayed at work. When the arbitrator's decision was received, the Rotherham uniform staff struck on

---

SHEFFIELD CORPORATION, L.M.S. & L.N.E. RAILWAYS. JOINT OMNIBUS COMMITTEE.
(Operated jointly with the Rotherham and Doncaster Corporation).

6847

ROUTE No. 77.

Sheffield - Rotherham - Doncaster

On and after Thursday, 1st October, 1942, by order of the Regional Transport Commissioner, the through service between Sheffield and Doncaster will be discontinued, and in future will operate between Rotherham and Doncaster only.

TIME TABLE from 1st OCTOBER, 1942.

Leave Rotherham for Doncaster—

Monday to Friday 8-30 a.m. and every hour until 9-30 p.m.

Saturday   8-30 a.m., 9-30, 10-0, 10-30, 11-0, 11-30 a.m. and every 20 minutes until 9-30 p.m.

Sunday   10-0 a.m. and every 30 minutes until 9-30 p.m.

Leave Doncaster for Rotherham—

Monday to Friday 8-30 a.m. and every hour until 9-30 p.m.

Saturday   8-30 a.m., 9-30, 10-0, 10-30, 11-0, 11-30 a.m. and every 20 minutes until 9-30 p.m.

Sunday   10-0 a.m. and every 30 minutes until 9-30 p.m.

Division Street,
    Sheffield, 1.   H. WATSON,
September, 1942.   Secretary.

The notice announcing for the second time that the Sheffield-Rotherham-Doncaster service was to close down – buses would run only from Rotherham to Doncaster.

Wednesday 12 May, actually against union advice. By Friday, 100 army lorries had been called in to cover for essential services. The Mexborough & Swinton staff also joined the strike on the Thursday. After a union meeting at which 144 members voted to start work again, some 23 against, the men returned to work on Tuesday 18 May, having gained nothing, but leaving a very discontented road staff. In the months following absenteeism by staff reached alarming figures. At times much of the early morning services had to be cancelled – no staff available. To increase the capacity of the single deck buses, on a number of them, the seating arrangement was altered to allow more standing passengers but there were now complaints that conductresses were sticking to the pre war "five only" standing rule – although 13 or 14 were now permitted. The fuel situation was still precarious and in 1943 there were no "holidays at home" coach trips into Derbyshire.

No 133 (AET 633, a Bristol J5G with a Cravens body joined the fleet in July 1937. During the war the first gas producer in Rotherham was fitted to this bus. The contraption is seen here in the depot yard. Gas producers were never very successful and all users were glad to see the back of them when no longer required. The white patches were to warn pedestrians not to pass behind the bus.

The Sheffield - Rotherham section of the route to Doncaster was closed from 1 October 1942. A gas producer unit was on order from the Bristol Company at a cost of £195. This was tried out on the Shenstone Road route in January 1943. The Ministry of Transport decided that Rotherham must use a further 5 sets - in September

two more units were available and these were used on Shenstone Road also.

In December 1943, the Deputy Manager, Mr Rylance, reported to his committee that, in January, eight Sunbeam trolley buses had entered service and that on the 14 November, the chassis frame on one had broken completely in two. There had been an inspection of this by a Ministry of War Transport engineer and it had been decided to replace all eight with frames to an improved design. Mr Rylance had taken over control of the department at the end of November when Mr Sykes became severely ill. Mr Sykes had been involved in a train accident in 1939 and had never fully recovered from its effects. He died on December 12 1943, He was 62 years old and already looking forward to retirement. When he came to Rotherham, just after the First World War, he took over a nearly derelict undertaking. He left it in the middle of the second world war as a prosperous and, in spite of the war, a very well maintained system. He will always be remembered for his belief in high speed single deck trolley buses, against the general tendency to operate double deck vehicles. Fifty years on and the single deck bus is becoming the norm in a very different world. Mr Rylance had been deputy manager from February 1943 and was promoted to Manager on February 1944 at a salary of £1,000 p.a. rising to £1,250.

Rotherham Corporation ⬥ **Transport Department**

WITHDRAWAL AND ALTERATION OF STOPPING PLACES.

Inward Trolley Bus Stop. **BOTTOM OF WELLGATE**
(Near Thickett's Shop)
Outward Tram Stop. **BOTTOM OF HIGH STREET**

Owing to increased congestion at the Junction of Wellgate and High Street, and the dangerous practice of intending passengers attempting to board moving tramcars at this point, it has been decided to withdraw the above-mentioned stopping places after Saturday, February 17th, 1945.

Commencing on Sunday, February 18th, Trolley Vehicles from Wickersley or Worry Goose Lane to Templeboro' will proceed through the Town Centre via All Saints' Square, Corporation Street, Howard Street, to the Tram Loading Barrier and thence by the normal route and through passengers will be allowed to remain on the vehicle.

Journeys from Templeboro' to Wickersley and Worry Goose Lane will continue to operate as at present.

Passengers are requested not to attempt to alight from Buses at the Traffic Lights at the bottom of High Street, nor to attempt to board Tramcars at this point.

MALTBY ROUTE.
Will passengers please note that from Sunday, February 18th, the inward and outward stops opposite 87, Rotherham Road, Maltby (near Leslie Avenue) will be moved one pole nearer Hellaby.

Transport Offices,
Frederick Street, Rotherham.
Feb. 13th, 1945.

N. RYLANCE, M. Inst. T.,
General Manager.

W. Taylor & Sons, Printers, Bridgegate.

An interesting notice issued by the new manager.

Newton Chambers of Chapeltown asked for a bus service from Rotherham to Roughwood Colliery in January 1943, and it was agreed to provide a service, on a month's trial with the consent of the Traffic Commissioners. It proved successful and was continued. The new Sunbeam frame members were to be delivered from April. It had been agreed that Rotherham staff would fit them at the Sunbeam Co.'s expense. The trolley bus reversing triangle at Flash Lane Bramley needed renewal. It was replaced by a new one at Cross Street, Bramley which would be a more convenient terminus. At the beginning of the war five obsolescent trolley buses had been stacked out of the way outside of the town. The new manager now doubted whether they would ever run again and he was authorised to dispose of them "as he deemed fit". In March 1944 Mr E Deakin of the Ipswich Transport Department was appointed to the post of Traffic Superintendent.

To cope with increasing traffic, older buses were being given heavy overhauls, three Bristols dating from 1931 with 4 cylinder diesel engines passed through the shops in 1944. They were given "modernised" bodies. A 1932 6 cylinder petrol engined Bristol had a particularly thorough rebuild at a cost of some £500 odd. Throughout the war, East Lancashire Coach builders had done body overhauls for Rotherham. Sample payments to them by Rotherham: In March 1943 - £488; November 1943 - £1,135 and January 1944 £693.

The new manager soon began to make changes. He immediately suggested that he preferred rear to centre entrance bodies and reported to his Committee on this in January and February 1945, but they were not yet ready for change and decided to take no action. In November 1944 he had already made a report on the Sheffield - Maltby service with which Sheffield and Rotherham held equal shares and Sheffield double deckers were altogether superior in capacity to the Rotherham vehicles. The Committee decided that he could convert 4 single deckers to double deckers at an estimated cost of £1,700 each, but in February 1945 he had to report that the Ministry of Supply would not allow the four buses to be converted but that, as one was damaged, that could be converted. Since four double deckers were needed, this was of little use and nothing was done, although the Ministry suggested that utility buses would be suitable inferring that these would be made available, but the offer was not taken up. Indeed Rotherham was one of the few undertakings which never owned a wartime utility bus.

In March 1944, it was agreed to place a "provisional" order for eight new trolley vehicle chassis - the maker was not specified, but East Lancashire Coachworks got the order for eight bodies. With the end of the war in Europe now in sight, many of the war time restrictions were lifted. In June 1945 permission was given for services to Worksop, Haworth, Bawtry & Roche Abbey and "the pre-war Sunday services" to be reinstated. The service to Haworth and Worksop started operation on Monday 1 October 1945. Later services were permitted and at Rotherham it was decided that last buses should be not later than 10.45 p.m.. Sheffield decided to operate the trams until 11.30 as from the 29 July, but Rotherham informed Sheffield that their last tram "for the present" would run at 11.00. Accordingly Sheffield cars only ran to Templeborough after 11.00. Trouble continued with trolley turning at Bessemer gates. With the end of the war, with peak services still turning here, Rotherham installed a light cluster to assist. There was a note issued on September 24 1945 "The lights are to switched "on" before and "off" after turning the trolley. Trouble still continued at the point. On September 1946, Mr Rylance wrote - again particularly about the 10.00 car to Intake. Two members of his Committee had complained to him that the car was lightly loaded at Bessemer and was not needed - particularly since it was followed by the 10.00 p.m. to Intake from Rotherham. At Sheffield it was felt that this car was still required in spite of the lighter loading after the end of the war, since the car picked up a full load before it reached Tinsley. The Committee members real complaint was that Sheffield could run extra trams for two or three people while Rotherham "could not run them for a decent load". Mr Rylance asked "as a personal favour if Sheffield would cut the tram out to help him"

After considering what was to be done about the Maltby - Sheffield service in September 1945, an order was placed with Bristol for 4 double deck chassis with East Lancashire bodies at a price of approximately £2,250 each. At the end of the year it was reported that the manager had disposed of three "bus ambulances" for £500. Armament work at the depot had already ceased by June 1945.

January 1946 began with the payment to East Lancashire of £860 for rebuilding a "bus body", followed by a further payment of £663 in March for "repairing coaches". Bristol received £2,381 in April for "spares and two bus chassis" and £2.430 in May for "chassis and parts". At this time the manager reported that he was having difficulty in getting new trolley buses "due to the authorised increase in width". In March the manager had reported that the

A strange end to a trolley bus body; No 30 a Ransome with Cravens body was new in 1931. When scrapped in 1945, the body was purchased by the South Yorkshire Navigation Co and fitted on to a canal barge. Any information as to its later history would be of interest.

Ministry of War Transport had allowed buses, and trolley vehicles, to be 8 foot wide – an increase of 6 inches on the previous maximum. He was authorised to enquire if the 12 vehicles on order could be built to the new dimensions, at which Rotherham Rural District Council decided that bottle necks on their road would have to be widened to take the 8 foot wide buses. This because it had been suggested that the new buses for the Sheffield – Maltby route should be to this width. At the March meeting of the Rotherham Council, a councillor proposed that double deck buses should be used on the Maltby route as far as Wickersley – particularly to reduce the congestion on the road between 5 and 6 p.m.. Alderman Caine said this, if implemented, would have the effect of reducing the existing frequency by a half. Double deck buses could not be run through to Maltby, because of the railway bridge. The platform staff were discontented with their rates of pay for Sunday work – Sheffield paid time and a half while Rotherham, in line

with similar Corporation transport operators, only paid time and a quarter. This particularly galled the Rotherham men working joint routes with Sheffield. On Sunday April 21 they came out on strike – no buses were run - additionally the joint routes from Sheffield to Maltby and to Doncaster had no service, whilst Mexborough & Swinton Traction Co. turned the trolley buses at the Stone Row boundary. Next Sunday, no agreement having been reached there was again no service. This continued for two months with little negotiation between the Corporation and the men. On the morning of the seventh Sunday of the strike, the "combatants" had a meeting which produced no agreement, after which the Corporation brought matters to a head by informing the men that any who did not turn up to work next Sunday would be dismissed. They did not, voting 190 to 17 to continue the strike, and accordingly the Corporation put up the dismissal notice and the men came out on the following Tuesday, Wednesday and Thursday. They gained nothing and returned to normal work on Friday, indeed the Mexborough & Swinton buses were already running into Rotherham on Thursday evening. There was a further application for the increase in August – which was refused and this time the men accepted the decision and there were no more strikes.

The excursions to Edwinstowe re- commenced on Sunday 6 July, the Regional Commissioners permitting 6 buses to be used on this service. In July the order for 8 AEC trolley bus chassis was cancelled and, instead, eight were ordered from Daimler with 7 ft 6 ins wide chassis to be fitted with English Electric equipment at a price of £2,375 each. Daimler hoped delivery of the chassis would commence in May 1947. In September 1946 the chairman reported that he and the Manager had been to Bristol, "to inspect the chassis" and had there and then increased the order from 6 to 12 chassis. The first of the double deck buses was received towards the end of 1946 and on the 9 December, Rotherham put the new buses on to the Sheffield - Maltby route, using three of the buses from Monday to Saturday. Only two were needed on Sundays. The four buses, Bristol K5G with 56 seat East Lancashire bodies were numbered 170/173 (DET 370/3). Charles Roberts of Wakefield now took orders for body repairs - in January 1947 they received £2,147 for overhauling and repairing buses. This was followed in March with £853 for repairs and overhaul of "a single deck" bus. In May a further £1,249 was paid to them for "overhauling and repairing a trolley bus". In February, Bristol had an order for 6 single deck chassis at £1,512 each for delivery in

March 1948. This was followed two months later with provisional orders for 6 double deck and 6 single deck chassis for delivery in 1949 and for 12 double deck and 6 single deck for 1950. The order for the whole of the bodies was to go to East Lancashire Coachbuilders. At the same time it was agreed to order 36 single deck trolley vehicles at 12 per annum for delivery in 1948; 1949 and 1950. This meant that, with the outstanding orders, the additions to the fleet would be 42 buses and 44 trolley vehicles.

No 9 FET 609 Paimler - East Lanes T.T.I.S 6.1550 withdrawn 8.1962 to Autospares 7.1963 renumber (1957) 45

Interior view showing seating arrangement. All cushions are the same height from the floor, including those over the wheel arches.

Centre entrance arrangement facilitates speedy loading of passengers.

Rotherham car No 5 moves on to the bridge over the canal by Bawtry Road. Preliminary work on the bridge replacement seems to be in progress. Because of this work, the through tram service was near its end. *Courtesy R J S Wiseman*

Tram No 18 standing in the Templeborough siding with the fields behind *Courtesy R. Mack*

Two cars at the Templeborough terminus, with the trolley bus wiring showing and a bus bound for Sheffield in the background.

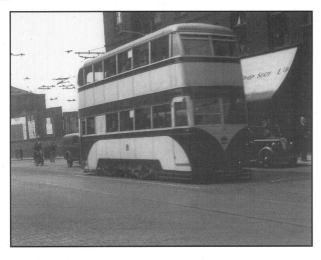

No. 11 in Westgate. The trolley bus wiring into Main St is behind the car.

A rear view of Tram No 11 passing down Corporation Street

No 9 on the curve from Frederick Street into Howard Street

No 11 entering the curve into High Street. *Photos Courtesy of D Packer*

The Templeborough tram route still needed maintenance and Dorman Long were paid £368 for new rails in 1946. In April 1947 Hadfields secured an order for "repair work, new crossings and points" at a cost of £939. The single ended trams were now showing the result of the heavy loading on the Sheffield road, and the need for rolling stock renewal was under consideration. Meanwhile Rotherham was short of cars, from January until April 1947 two cars a week were taken on loan from Sheffield. A total of 62 different cars were provided, mainly from Tinsley and Shoreham Street tram depot stocks. The cars were stacked overnight in the Rawmarsh Road depot, which looked quite strange with the Sheffield cars standing in the forecourt for which a new track layout was being designed. In October 1947, Hadfields tender of £1,052 for this work was accepted. There was further expenditure on the tramway, in June 1948 Dorman Long received £400 for new tram rails. In October, Leeds Corporation was paid £30 for tram No 14 which had been taken on loan during the war. On 1 September 1947, Mr Rylance wrote to the Sheffield manager with a copy of his instructions to drivers whilst track relaying was in progress over Bow Bridge. In November 1947 a Rotherham employee wrote a note to the Traffic Superintendent with objections to Sheffield trams which were running late being turned at various points – short of Rotherham – often without instructions from inspectors. In fact passengers had been turned off at Westgate and had to walk the rest of the way into town. In the correspondence between the two operators it was pointed out that, in the event of a serious hold up when a Rotherham tram had to be reversed it never carried passengers in this position. Mr Rylance, when closing the correspondence, finished his letter with the sentence "I might mention that it is a dangerous practice to turn a Rotherham tram back at some point because it

College Square in 1949 with trams still running to Templeborough; A
Sheffield bus on its return journey to the city. Also one of the first Bristol
double deck buses of 1946 with an East Lancs Body.
Courtesy Quadrant Picture Library, Sutton, Surrey

necessitates the vehicle travelling backwards to
Rotherham and the passengers have to get off at the
driver's end. This of course is no fault of yours, neither is
it any fault of mine. The trams were put into operation
before my arrival in Rotherham." So much for the
erstwhile "Pride of Rotherham".

At this time, preparatory work was in progress by the
Sheffield City Engineers Department, for the removal of
the old bridge over the railway and canal between Vulcan
Road and Bawtry Road on the way to Rotherham.
At first it was thought to do the work "in halves" with a
temporary single track on each side of the old and new
bridges, as necessary, until completion. However, it was
decided to close the bridge to tram traffic during
reconstruction and provide a temporary bus service. The
through tram route between the two towns closed on
Saturday 11 December 1948. Although not yet
confirmed, the last Sheffield tram to Templeborough had
been run - the through tram service never returned. At
Rotherham, with insufficient double deck buses yet
available and a large amount of money required for new
track already on order or received - but not now required,
there was not a little difficulty. For a time the single
ended cars shuttled between College Square and
Templeborough but the "writing was on the wall". Early
in the morning of 1 April 1949, two trams collided "head
on" outside Steel Peech & Tozers' Ickles Gate and both
were extensively damaged. The cab on one car was
completely wrecked - although both cars were driven to
Rawmarsh Road under their own power. It is doubtful if
they ever ran again. If they were repaired they would
hardly have entered service before the end of
tram operation.

In July 1949 it was agreed that, as soon as possible when
buses were available, the tram route should be
abandoned. It was also agreed to discontinue the trolley
bus service to Templeborough. It was noted that therefore
the through trolley bus services direct to Templeborough
from Worry Goose Lane, Thrybergh and Kilnhurst Road
would cease. These must have been "peak hour" services
which never appeared in the public timetables - as did
that from Maltby. The reference to Kilnhurst Road
suggest that possibly the Mexborough & Swinton
Tramways Co trolley buses ran through from here to
Templeborough, as they certainly did to Ferham Road for
football matches at Millmoor. It was decided to sell the
substation equipment from the route at once. It is
assumed that the trolley bus service also closed down at
that time, but apart from the reference to it in the July
meeting, it was not mentioned again. In Corporation
records, it is listed as "November 1949", presumably when
the trams ceased running, the power was turned off.

The last Rotherham tram ran on Sunday 13 November
1949. The long warfare between the two towns was over.
Relations were now friendly and Sheffield loaned
Rotherham five double deck buses, Nos. 483, 488 to 491
- for the period until further Rotherham double deck
buses, already on order, should be received. The Sheffield
buses were wartime "utility" vehicles with Weymann
bodies and Guy Arab II chassis with Gardner 6 L W
engines of a type never seen before in the Rawmarsh
Road depot. Presumably Sheffield covered any major
maintenance which may have been required. It was not
until April 1949 that the much needed new Rotherham
Crossley's were received and the Sheffield buses returned.
The accompanying letter to Sheffield's Mr R C Moore
finished with the sentence "May I take the opportunity of
thanking you for the assistance you have given since the
12 December, as without such assistance I could not have
done my share of the Rotherham to Sheffield service.
With kind regards, N Rylance". Truly a new period had
commenced. The single end cars were offered to Sheffield
and a truck that had been removed was inspected. The
result of the cars running in only one direction was
obvious. The flange on the near front corner was
practically non existent, being almost in the running face
centre and only about $1/2$ inch of the flange remained.
These trucks were not of a pattern used by Sheffield and
no interest was shown, but much of the equipment which
could be used, including the new track work, was
purchased and taken into Sheffield stock.

The long term effects of war shortages and the post war stringency were ending and expansion was once again in the air. In the Thrybergh area housing development was already in progress in the Vale Road area, to which it will be recalled, the Rotherham Rural District Council had prevented the Thrybergh trolley buses travelling through the section. Now additional transport was required and, as a start, in October 1946 it was decided to re-route the Haworth service, between Rotherham and Silverwood, through the area - the buses to Worksop had been using the route via Doncaster Road, Park Lane, Vale Road and Hollings Lane since September 1932. Trolley bus extensions were still possible and in February 1947 the Town Clerk was requested to ask for a further extension of the time allowed for the routes in the 1937 Act, due to expire in October 1948. At this time the manager recommended an extension of the trolley bus route from Colin Campbell for a further 5/8ths of a mile to the Old Toll Bar at Wortley Road, to assist with traffic being generated by new housing in this area also.

The Ministry of Transport at last issued the licence, in June 1947, for the joint service with the East Midlands Co from Rotherham to Chesterfield by way of Swallownest. At the same time they were authorised once again to operate the Sunday "excursion" service to Gunthorpe Bridge which recommenced on 22 June. In the month, Sheffield United Tours were paid £18.18.0d for the hire of coaches. This was followed in September with licences for the joint service with East Midland to Worksop via Dinnington and, locally, for a new route to East Herringthorpe, where additional houses were being built, "when the roads were completed". The East Herringthorpe route was opened on 15 December 1947, but commencement of the joint service to Worksop and Chesterfield, hoped to start in July, was held up by negotiations with the East Midland Co. Both routes finally commenced on 4 January 1948, in the case of the Chesterfield route, some 10 years after it was first discussed.

The short extension from the Colin Campbell opened on 2 May 1948 after land had been purchased for a turning circle. At the same time it was also decided to buy a plot of land for a turning circle at Ewers Road to do away with the trolley bus reversing triangle, which was proving a nuisance. This was brought into use early in 1949. Other additions to the trolley vehicle overhead in the year from March 1948 had been the construction at the junction of Rawmarsh Road and Chantry Bridge of a further turning circle here for the Greasbrough trolley buses. At the same time a separate pair of wires had been installed in Frederick Street for the Rawmarsh & Mexborough buses. With the closure of the Templeborough route, the wiring around the tight bend into All Saints Square, used by the buses from Maltby, was removed.

In January 1950, a Barnsley "breaker" offered £420 for the tramcar bodies only and was accepted. The trucks and electrical equipment got no reference - possibly the Corporation broke them up and sold the scrap. It was agreed to take up the tram track to allow for alterations between the top of High Street and Main Street and in September it was agreed to pay the Highways Department the sum of £26,010 for removing the rails and "making good" - getting rid of the trams proved expensive.

On the bus side, further alterations were made. - the Sheffield - Maltby route was extended from the Queen's Hotel, along Miglet Lane as far as the junction of Victoria Street and Outgang Lane - at a penny fare addition. A month later it was decided to extend the Brinsworth service into the new Brinsworth housing estate.

Views of the Greasbrough trolley bus route in 1950

Just leaving the Musbrough Lane stop. There was a short journey turning loop here; the third set of wires and the junction frog can be seen.

Further along towards Greasbrough

A trolley bus on the loop round the terminal roads

Trolley bus No 9 (FET 609) standing at the Greasbrough terminus

In January 1951 an application was made to the Traffic Commissioners for permission to extend the Worry Goose Lane route as far as Sitwell Park Gate. More momentous it was decided to convert the Greasbrough trolley bus route to motor buses "to reduce costs". There had been a loss on the trolley bus operation of £16,916 in the year ended March 1950 followed by one of over £11,000 next year - but it was mentioned that this included "accrued expenditure" on the old tram system, without splitting them up. In March 1950 it had been noted that since the "take-over" of the Electricity Undertaking by the British Electricity Authority, the average price of Electricity had risen from 6.3d to 6.5d. So not only had the town lost - at no financial return - its profitable electricity department, the transport charge had increased. By the year end March 1954 the department was paying 9.3d per unit. When the Greasbrough trolley buses ceased to operate, probably on May 4th or 5th, it was noted in the press that the change

from trolley buses to "petrol" buses was due to the rising costs of electricity now it is nationalised. The date of the Greasbrough conversion never seems to have been published, though the Traffic Commissioners authorised the change on May 4th. A year later in the issue of a local newspaper for May it was noted that it was just over a year ago that the changeover took place. It was then mentioned that all the standards and electrical equipment from Greasbrough and Worry Goose Lane which, using double decker buses, was converted on July 2 1951, was now being removed and that as much as possible would be re-used. Incidentally, a newspaper comment dated June 9 1951 was that the Greasbrough residents had liked their smooth trolley buses and were already regretting the change.

There was a profit on the buses of £10,000 for the year end March 1951 - which did not cover the loss on the trolley vehicle operation. At this stage it was realised that to cover the increasing operating costs it would finally be necessary to apply for a fare increase. Rotherham had managed to keep its fares unchanged for some 25 years, probably a record for the country. There had been a post war boom with increasing passenger totals but this was changing rapidly. The manager particularly referred to the increasing use by the population of their own transport, and the decline was rapid. In the previous few years there had been some rather odd fleet renumbering according to year of manufacture - at the year end March 1948, the trolley buses had all been numbered according to year of manufacture and into type groups, the bus fleet followed next year. From personal experience, nothing can cause so much trouble with so little gain. In any case a few years after renumbering the situation is where you were, with new vehicles in the fleet and older buses still surviving. In 1951 a new colour scheme was decided on - the dark blue livery was replaced by a pale azure blue which, though the new manager was possibly not aware of the fact, was not dissimilar to the original colour scheme of the despised and long forgotten single end cars.

The fare increase was agreed in June 1951, when it was decided to discontinue the provision of prepaid and discount tickets. The new Sitwell Park Gate extension of the Worry Goose bus route was not proving profitable and it was agreed to ask the Traffic Commissioners for authority to halve the Sitwell Park Gate service and make a new terminus at Cowrakes Lane in Whiston for the other half.. There had been changes in the Badsley Moor Lane area services. In April 1951 an advertisement appeared in the local papers, by Rotherham Transport

Department, announcing that from May 28 the existing long established East Dene route would be discontinued, to be replaced by services to Far Lane, with a terminus at East Dene Hotel, and to Tennyson Road by the existing route along Badsley Moor Lane to Browning Road and along Tennyson Road to Far Lane and finally extending the existing Chaucer Road route to the roundabout at the end of Browning Road. The Chaucer Road route had opened on January 12 1951. The new service to Tennyson Road had been granted by the Traffic Commissioners on March 5 1951, that for the route on Cowrakes Lane as far as Park Avenue in Whiston on November 16 1951.

It was not until March 1951 that Fullerton Road substation, not required after the closure of the Templeborough tram route, was dismantled and the rectifying equipment sold to the Mexborough & Swinton Traction Co. Similarly the substation material from both Worry Goose Lane and Greasbrough was not removed until 1953 to be re-used in the town centre substation, at the Power Station, in replacement of the old rotary converter equipment. During 1953, the overhead wiring at the Pumping Station was improved while some of the layout on the curves on the Dalton section were adjusted to reduce de-wirements on the route. These were the "bane" of trolley bus operation - the fact that the buses could deviate was always given as an advantage over rail bound vehicles - but the results of "deviating" could be trolleys off, while dewirements at overhead frogs in the town centre could be disastrous. Replacement of trolley poles after a dewirement could prove hazardous for the uniform staff. In August 1955 a conductor was killed by a lorry running into him at the rear of the bus as he helped the driver replace the trolleys after a dewirement at Listerdale on the Maltby section. There had been a similar fatality in 1942 when the driver of a trolley bus was killed - being struck by a following Silverwood bus as he attempted to replace the trolleys.

The first fare increase did not produce the desired result and a year later, in June 1952, it was agreed to apply for an increase in the normal fares of a halfpenny more on fares under 8d and a penny on all fares over 8d. As a "softener" to the blow a series of 1d stages were introduced. The new estates were needing bus services and in July 1953 a service into Kimberworth Park Estate was proposed. There was no suggestion now of extending the Kimberworth trolley buses into the estate. Instead the new route duplicated it at its outer end and the whole trolley bus section from Ewers Road turning circle to the Toll Bar was discontinued on 28 September 1953 and the

overhead material removed immediately. The new Kimberworth Park Estate route ran from the Chantry Bridge in Rotherham by way of College Road and Midland Road to Roughwood Road and its junction with Bents Road. The application to the Traffic Commissioners for authority to provide the service was dated July 17 1953. The Rotherham terminus was unsuitable and on October 23 was moved up to Bridgegate. Next year the route was extended to Oxclose Avenue.

Trolley buses between Wickersley and Maltby in the final days of trolley bus operation during 1954.

Wickersley short working terminus, with a bus running through from Maltby.

Leaving Maltby for Wickersley.

Extensions were being needed at Maltby to serve new housing. The Sheffield and Maltby route had already been extended from the Queens Hotel trolley bus terminus to Victoria Street in April 1950. In September 1954 it was decided to convert the section of the Maltby route between Wickersley and Maltby from the single deck trolley bus operation to double deck diesel engined buses. From the Queens Hotel extensions were to be provided for some half a mile along Grange Lane into the

Manor Housing Estate, and southerly along Miglet Lane to the Model Village Estate. A revised fare scale was proposed with an extra penny to the new termini. The change took place on 3 May 1954 leaving the department with far too many trolley buses for service requirements. In June the Kimberworth Park route, No 38, via the Toll Bar was again extended along West Close as far as Bents Road, while No 39 via Bradgate was also to be extended from the existing terminus in Barber Balk Road to terminate in Northern Road. The Hellaby substation, now redundant, was dismantled and the equipment sold to "another municipality" - not named in the Committee minutes. On Christmas Eve 1954, the manager, Mr N Rylance was taken ill at a dinner dance at Doncaster and died. He was only 56 years old, had started his transport career at Bolton, become traffic superintendent at Wigan and came in that capacity to Rotherham under Mr Sykes. During his period of office he had seen the change from a prosperous department to one with declining receipts and ever increasing costs. He had had to arrange for fare increases to prevent operating at a loss and after one short extension of the trolley bus section, had started the gradual changeover to diesel bus operation. The changes he had made since the "Sykes era" were distinct. During Sykes' "reign", Rotherham had been "different" with its single deck fleet and centre entrance bodies. From the moment the first new double deck buses entered the fleet, it joined the national post war "normal". As developments took place, Rotherham followed the trend - similar vehicles could be seen running in any British town. The Corporation had lost its electricity department and the trolley buses no longer used "home produced" and reasonably cheap power. Diesel operation was cheaper and the possible advantage of speed and comfort was no longer of great importance.

One of the 1930 Daimler/East Lancs trolley buses No 20 (FET 620) passes under the Hellaby railway bridge on its journey from Maltby to Rotherham. The bridge was too low for the double deck trolley buses and was one of the reasons for the conversion to bus operation of the section from Wickersley to Maltby. *Photo courtesy late R Bower.*

No 87 (FET 347) on the turning circle at Maltby

CHAPTER 2

Years of Change

Mr I O Fisher, the Traffic Superintendent immediately took over the management functions, but at the Committee meeting the appointment of a new manager was deferred until the February one when Mr Fisher was confirmed in his post as manager from 1 March 1955. Since he had been in Rotherham for some years he was already aware of the department's strengths and weaknesses - and equally he knew the Rotherham district and was not a newcomer having to "find his feet". In July he issued a report on the losses being incurred by the trolley bus section and he proposed that 14 of the latest six wheel single deck trolley buses should have the chassis overhauled and adjusted to make them available to be fitted with double deck bodies. A Doncaster Corporation six wheel double deck trolley bus was borrowed in June 1955 to check the suitability of the Rotherham overhead wiring to accommodate double decker buses. This was successful and in September the Park Royal tender for 14 double deck bodies at £2,736 each was accepted. This was not the first double deck trolley bus to be tried out at Rotherham – twenty years previously, Mr Sykes, acting as consultant on behalf of the Cape Town Tramways Company, in 1935 had been responsible for testing one of the first of that Company's new fleet of trolley buses. One of them, A Ransome with a Weymann's body, was tried out at Rotherham for the official road test – over a route 8.9 miles long – probably from Kimberworth to Thrybergh particularly to check the hill climbing. There was no suggestion that the overhead needed any alteration and if the new manager had been informed, possibly the experiment with the Doncaster double deck bus would not have taken place.

On 15 June 1955, a Doncaster trolley bus was borrowed to test the Rotherham overhead wiring which had been installed for use with single deck vehicles. The test proved that double deck trolley buses could be used at Rotherham – though in places the existing wiring had to be lifted as much as 2 feet.

On test near the top of Old Gate Hill at Thrybergh
Courtesy of Mr Warnes

The rear view shows the overhead at the junction between the Thrybergh and Silverwood Colliery routes

Doncaster trolley bus No 363 (BDT 127) standing in the Rawmarsh Road depot entrance yard

Receipts were still not keeping up with expenditure and the decline in passengers continued at what had become an alarming rate. A further fare increase was agreed in December 1955, again 1/2d on single fares up to 5d, a penny on those of 6d and over and the 1 1/2d stages were to be withdrawn. However it was realised that each fare increase would cause further losses of passengers carried, indeed in his annual report for year end March 1957, Mr Fisher in his comments on the financial position noted that the reduction in passengers carried in that year was some 1,700,000 more than for 1956, and that people were now using their cars to work.

In the first year of the new manager's "tenancy", there were few changes in the operations field. Delivery was taken of five low height double deck buses which were used to convert the Treeton route from single to double deck operation on 12 September 1955. These buses were the last to be ordered under Rylance's managership in December, a few weeks before his death. The first two of the new double deck trolley buses were delivered in March 1956 and one was tried out between Kimberworth, Thrybergh and Silverwood at once. Sufficient were delivered to allow the new service to commence on Monday May 5. It was pointed out that the new 70 seat buses carried nearly twice as many passengers as the old single deck deckers. The service frequency was reduced, but it was noted that, because of these changes, there were more seats per hour available for passengers - but they had to wait longer between buses. However the manager was very pleased with the financial result - a loss of nearly £12,000 on the trolley buses in the year to March 31 1956 was converted into a profit of £13,800 for 1957. In the last 28 days prior to the conversion, the single deck service had provided a revenue of 31.8 pence per mile. for the first 28 days of the double deck service this had risen to 42.2 pence per mile. The change was so successful that a further 6 of the single deckers were converted and used for the conversion of the Wickersley route to double deck operation on 6 February 1957. The remaining single deck trolley buses in the fleet were only needed for the joint service to Mexborough and a number lay out of use in the depot. It was noted that, for the conversion the overhead had to be raised in places by as much as 2 feet.

One of the double deck trolley buses standing in All Saints Square before starting on its journey to Pumping Station on the Thrybergh route where there was an elaborate turning loop. *Courtesy A B Cross*

The manager was continually being asked for additional services and "odd" extra buses at peak times, particularly from the Rotherham Rural District villages, but in the prevailing financial climate, most of these requirements could only have been provided at a loss. However, after

quite strong requests from miners living in a new estate at Sunnyside, a service was provided from 23 October 1956 between the village and Silverwood colliery - at shift times. In July of that year, double deck buses replaced the single deckers on the joint routes - Sheffield and Doncaster and between Rotherham and Worksop by way of Dinnington - on which route, before the changeover could be implemented, much heavy tree lopping was required. Also, between Laughton Post Office and Laughton Common the lamp standards had to be raised to clear the top decks.

At this stage the complete conversion from trolley bus to diesel bus was not being considered, in fact in June 1956, in response to requests for extensions, a letter from the Rotherham management to the Thrybergh Parish Council informed that body that a trolley vehicle extension from Park Lane to the new housing estate at Vale Road was then under consideration. It did not happen, the last extension of the trolley bus system was already in the past.

The decline in the number of passengers carried continued, nearly 2½ million in the year ended March 1958 and 1½ million next year. From being a prosperous undertaking, costs were barely covering receipts and a further fare increase was needed, although in 1958 five buses were purchased out of revenue. As larger buses were purchased, service frequencies continued to decline - though the number of seats available per hour did increase - a great help at peak load times, On the Greasbrough route on 2 December 1957 new 44 seat single deck buses were provided with an immediate service reduction. The only service additions were to the new housing estates - in August 1958 a service from Bridgegate to Rhodes Avenue in the Kimberworth Park Estate was provided. In Jan 1961 the route was extended from the Rhodes Avenue terminus to Oaks Lane - this time with an increased frequency. Ever since the passing of the Road Traffic Act in the 1930s, the use of one man operated buses had been restricted to buses seating 26 or less passengers. Now, with changing circumstances this restriction was removed - so far as large capacity single deck buses were concerned. At Rotherham, the new development was welcomed by management - less so by the transport unions. The department decided that the long loss making routes to Harworth and Worksop would be ideal ones for an experiment and, during a week in July 1960, there were two "test" runs to Worksop under one man operation. After much negotiation it was finally agreed in November to experiment with the system, but with the reservation that only on the section of the route from Maltby to Haworth and Worksop. It was not stated what happened to the conductor when he was dropped at Maltby. It is not thought that the service was frequent enough to allow him to pick up a bus at Maltby returning to Rotherham. The agreement included the clause that only volunteers would be asked to work this one man route - nobody volunteered! In spite of some protest from regular passengers on the route, it was decided that it could no longer be operated under existing conditions. Accordingly, an application was made to the Traffic Commissioners to abandon licences for Rotherham to Harworth and to Worksop. The application when made also included that from Rotherham to Bawtry and the services were withdrawn from 1 October 1961. The bus service between Rotherham and Bawtry had commenced in the early 19th Century - and was probably one of the longest lived services of this type, without a break, in Britain.

The year ending March 31 1960 saw, for the first time in some years, the end for the time being of the decline in number of passengers carried by an increase of over 400,000. This was in spite of a further decline in trolley bus passengers - but it should be realised that motor buses now ran along the remaining trolley bus routes and were carrying passengers who would previously have been using the trolley vehicles. It was not known what caused the welcome change since private car numbers continued to increase. The greatest change during the year was caused by the general introduction of the 42 hour working week and the times of peak loading altered. Because of the considerable wage awards which had been estimated to cost some £46,000 a year, another application for fare increases had been made. These were increased again in June 1961 - 1/2d on fares from 31/2d to 81/2d, one penny from 9d to 1/-d with 2d on fares over 11/2d. As a point of interest it was noticed that the cost of interest on remaining loans, £9,306, was greater than the interest being received on departmental investments, so the loan was paid off out of revenue. There were now only 20 single deck motor buses in the fleet with 93 double deck buses whilst the 20 double deck trolley buses covered most of the trolley vehicle operation. There were still 23 single deck trolley buses in stock for which there was little need - apart from Rotherham's small share of provision for the Mexborough service.

The Mexborough & Swinton Traction Co withdrew trolley buses from the Rotherham to Conisbrough route on Monday 27 March 1961. The replacements were double deck diesel engined buses, Rotherham providing

Towards the end of trolley bus operation to Mexborough, Rotherham trolley bus FET 336, originally No 76, travels along Warren Vale road "out in the country".

Long after the last trolley bus had been run in Rotherham, many from the fleet continued their life in Spain. Here is one at Cadiz. Before leaving Rotherham they were reconditioned. It is not known whether the centre exit was moved to the "continental" side by Rotherham as part of the contract

similar vehicles for its share of the joint route after some acrimonious negotiations between Corporation and Company which will be detailed in the Mexborough & Swinton Traction Co chapter. With the closure of the Mexborough & Swinton Co route there was no possible use for the single deck trolley buses at Rotherham. After an agreement had been made to sell them to a Spanish operator, 17 of them were reconditioned at Rotherham before their despatch. The overhead wiring in the Corporation area between Stone Row Boundary - the erstwhile Greasbrough boundary and the Rawmarsh Road depot was removed. Though they were only of use for depot working, the single pair of wires along Rawmarsh Road to Chantry Bridge was retained for possible emergency use.

Apart from the changes due to the Mexborough & Swinton Co 's abandonment of its trolley bus system, the only alterations at Rotherham were due to the continuing

Corporation Street before the demise of the trolley buses. No 44 (FET 618) with its Roe double deck body was originally no 18 with an East Lancs single deck body.

Trolley buses on the Brecks turning circle in the final years of trolley bus operation on the remaining portion of the erstwhile Maltby route. *Courtesy A D Packer*

Buses in Bridgegate looking up to All Saints Square. Bus No 200 (FET 354) a Bristol with East Lancs body dates from 1949 while the bus pulling out, a Daimler with a Roe Body (No 76. CET 76C) was new in 1965. Buses were still running to Templeborough.

expansion of the outer area housing developments. In October 1961 it was agreed to extend the existing Chaucer Road route (No 13) from its terminus along Browning Road and Herringthorpe Valley Road to Dovedale Road, passing along Dovedale Road as far as Dale Road which it also followed to Farfield Road. It continued along Farfield Road to a new temporary terminus area near to Athron Drive on that road. However, it was not until 12 August 1962 that the extension was made. On the 30 May 1960 the Catcliffe route had been altered between Canklow and White Hill, to pass along Brinsworth Lane and White Hill Road. To assist with the Brinsworth loading, the Canklow service was extended in August 1961 along Brinsworth Lane as far as the Three Magpies Hotel. The extension to Farfield Road proved unremunerative and accordingly on 17 December 1962 it was cut back to a terminus at Dovedale Road at its junction with Herringthorpe Valley Road but with an additional and separate service, approximately half hourly to Fairfield Road on weekdays. In November 1962 it was agreed to change the Richmond Park service

to Poucher Street. In 1962 there were some major alterations to the roads around Effingham Square and the complicated overhead installation here was completely reconstructed. After this Silverwood buses passed through the town centre and All Saints Square and were provided with a terminus in Corporation Street. At the same time a shunt was again installed at Davy's Corner by All Saints Square, which allowed trolley buses from Wickersley to travel through All Saints Square to reach the depot.

The year 1963 commenced with the trolley bus service to Brecks and Wickersley being converted from the 14 January to diesel bus operation, leaving only the Kimberworth, Thrybergh and Silverwood routes served by trolley buses. In June the Manager was asked to provide a bus service to the Wingfield estate which was being built on the stretch of land between Greasbrough and the Thorpe Hesley Road. He decided that, since the last section of the Greasbrough route in the village was operated at a loss, this should be terminated at the Cross

Inn in Greasbrough and re-routed from here via the Coach Road, Forton Wood and Roughwood Road and along Wingfield Road to a terminus in the middle of the new estate. The change took place from 21 October 1963, but not before the residents on the truncated section at Greasbrough had protested vigorously at the proposed loss of their buses, particularly since the service to Greasbrough was not so good as in the trolley bus period. Before the changeover took place, it was agreed that a half hourly service would be given to Wingfield with a similar service to the old Greasbrough terminus, thus providing a quarter hour interval service as far as the Crown Inn

In November 1964 it was decided that the last trolley bus route from Kimberworth (Ewer's Road) to Thrybergh and the Silverwood colliery branch should be converted to diesel bus operation when the new buses on order, due for delivery in September 1965, were received. In September 1965 it was agreed to fix a "target" date for the conversion of Sunday 3 October 1965.

Scenes on the last trolley bus route "Kimberworth to Thrybergh & Silverwood - *all courtesy P J Thompson*.

Kimberworth, the Ewers Road turning circle.

Kimberworth, Ferham Road corner from Coronation Bridge

Silverwood terminus with No 6 (FET 610) on an enthusiasts tour.

A sylvan scene on the Silverwood branch.

Near to the Silverwood Colliery terminus.

The last trolley bus ran on 2 October 1965 with little ceremony - apart from "last trolley bus" tours by two different trolley bus museum society members. Each of them wished to run the last trolley bus so, after some discussion, the two parties joined together for the last run. Each society, the National Trolley Bus Association and the Nottingham Trolley Bus Society were presented with one of the vehicles by the Corporation - thus preserving part of Rotherham's transport history at no further cost to the Corporation.

Thrybergh terminus with turning circle overhead wiring in the background.

The intricate wiring at Mowbray Street. It was to this point at the "Pumping Station" that the first trams ran in 1903.

The junction at the top of Oldgate Hill between the Thrybergh and Silverwood sections. No 31 (FET 615) is coming down from Thrybergh.

The junction wiring at the Rotherham end of Fitzwilliam Road.

A trolley bus passing down Old Gate Hill

Frederick Street with the site cleared for the bus station in October 1965. A Mexborough and Swinton Atlantean, No 2, is passed by Rotherham trolley bus No 42 on its way to Thrybergh.
Courtesy P J Thompson

There were some route alterations for the replacing services. The through route from Thrybergh (Park Lane) to Kimberworth (Colin Campbell) continued to Richmond Park, while from Pumping Station to Kimberworth Park went via the Toll Bar. In the annual report for the year end (1965/66) the manager commented " The abandonment of the trolley buses is a major change in operation and reluctant as one is to see these grand vehicles disappear from our streets it was no longer economical to retain them."

In October 1964 there had been changes in the circular route serving Far Lane and Tennyson Road. This was discontinued and converted to separate routes with the Tennyson Road route terminating at Goldsmith Road. At the beginning of November, Howard Street in the town centre was changed to a one way road and services into town from Westgate were diverted up High Street and College Street to All Saints Square. On 6 January at the Maltby end of the Sheffield route, Miglet Lane ceased to be used , buses travelling along the Tickhill Road to the National Coal Board estate with a terminus at Quilter Road. In February 1965 it was reported that the long standing Sundays excursions, mostly for fishermen, had ceased to be profitable. It was agreed to apply to the Traffic Commissioners for permission to close the operation. They were withdrawn in April. A rather strange request was made in April 1966 for a "feeder" service between Masborough railway station and the bus station, but in June it was decided that such a service would be quite impractical. In July it was reported that the peak demand on the Wingfield Estate service, of necessity using single deck buses, was only being met with difficulty. It was suggested that to allow double deck buses to be used, they should be routed along College Road and Fenton Road to obviate the need for buses to pass under the low railway bridge on the Greasbrough Road. The suggestion was accepted in principle and from January 1967 the peak bus service - to a separate route service number - was diverted. At the same time the Wingfield Estate route was extended to a new terminus. Once again a further increase in fares was becoming necessary but in August it was decided not to make an application, but to consider service reduction to save expenditure. Finally in November 1966 it was agreed that there would have to be an application for a further fare increase. At the same time the Transport Ministry decided to increase the possibility of one man operation, by permitting the top deck of buses to be sealed off allowing the buses to be used, in effect, as one man single deck vehicles. It was noted that front entrance buses were essential for one man operation. In June an order had been passed to Daimler for 9 forward engined chassis and 3 Fleetline chassis with rear engines. Next month the order was amended to be for 12 rear engined chassis. For some years the All Saints Square terminus had no longer been large enough for the traffic while alterations to the town centre, with proposals for one way traffic, had made moves to a new site necessary. A covered bus station was now required and a site on the old Gas Works premises off Frederick Street was selected. The plans for the bus station received council approval in November 1964 – by the following October construction of the transport office department was so far advanced that plans for an early move were discussed. The transport office was finally moved from the municipal offices on Monday 14 March 1966. This was followed on 6 January 1967 with the opening of the bus station site. From this date the buses gradually used the area as a terminus, although it was some years before building was completed and the bus station was ready for the official opening. Three "new" routes used the station from this date, No 54 to Greasbrough via Potter Hill, No 55 to Wingfield, also by way of Potter Hill and No 56 to Wingfield via College Road and Fenton Road.

In February 1967 Shardlows asked for a work people's service from the Wingfield Estate to their works at Blackburn. The manager was asked to make a report on the request but there is no record of the report being produced. However in April, Mr Fisher reported to the Committee that he intended to retire on 30 June 1967.

It was not until December that his final annual report for the year ended 31 March 1967 was published. Basically they had carried a million passengers less than the previous year while there was a trading deficit of some £45,000. He commented "The time is coming and the portents are that before very long decisions will be taken which will direct or encourage the reversion to public transport which most people will agree is the solution to many of the problems caused by congestion in our towns" …. " my hope is that the decision will not be too long delayed".

Unfortunately that sentence could still be written in 1999.

CHAPTER 3

Mexborough & Swinton Traction Co

The Company entered the war with the trolley bus fleet dating from 1926 - 30, whilst the three petrol buses Nos. 1 - 3 were far from new. Nos. 1 & 2 were Dennis Darts with London Lorries 20 seater bodies dating from 1933. No 3, a Leyland PLSC 3 with a Brush 30 seat body which had been acquired by the Mexborough Company in 1935 from the Yorkshire Traction Co was new in 1928. During 1939 a further second hand petrol engined bus, No 91 (CP 6546) was bought from the Hebble Co, an Albion with a 30 seat body, which dated from April 1928. The petrol engined routes were an unimportant part of the Mexborough & Swinton operations. The original Mexborough and Goldthorpe service had been taken over by the Yorkshire Traction Co on 3 May 1930. This left only routes between Low Stubbin Village and Kilnhurst, opened on 25 April 1925 and a Friday and Saturday afternoon service from Greasbrough to Kilnhurst which had been commenced on 10 June 1927.

As at Rotherham, icy road conditions during the first winter of the war was the cause of very serious damage to the buses. By February 1940 some half of the fleet was stuck in the depot either under repair or standing until they could be taken in hand. In the issue of the Rotherham Advertiser for Saturday 10 February the Company, in an advertisement, regretted the inconvenience to passengers at first for the irregular service and finally the complete suspension of operation of the trolley bus routes from Rotherham to Conisbrough and Manvers Main to Conisbrough. It was noted that Rotherham Corporation had been able to operate as far as Parkgate on the previous Tuesday, while it was hoped that the Mexborough services would start again on the Wednesday. There was also a note in a local newspaper dated Saturday, February 10 1940 that the through service on the Rotherham to Conisbrough trolley bus route was run yesterday "and will continue". In the next week's Advertiser, the Mexborough company again apologised for the irregular services, now because of staff shortage due to sickness. The public were informed that services would have to be curtailed at peak times from Saturday 27 February.

Once the winter was over, the services returned to the wartime normal. Since the petrol bus routes were of minor importance, there had been few service reductions at the start of the war. The Kilnhurst route, which had

been extended from the "Co-op" as far as Denaby Lane in 1937, was moved back to the old "Co-op" terminus in January 1940. In August Rawmarsh Council was glad to support the Company in its application for permission to make a turning circle at the junction of Dale Road and Kilnhurst Road, where the Green Lane route joined the Rotherham - Mexborough route. In March 1941 the directors authorised the purchase of a "third hand" single deck bus from the Yorkshire Traction Co for £350. This was an Albion "Victor" vehicle AWR 887 with a 30 seat body by a local firm, Barnsley Bodies. It had been new to a small proprietor, Mr McAdoo of Cudworth in 1935 and passed to Yorkshire Traction in October 1940 before joining the Mexborough fleet as No 76. On 7 April 1941 a war emergency petrol bus service was provided between Kilnhurst and Milton Street, Swinton between 4 and 6 p.m. each day. Next year from 17 September a further trip was added at 2.00 p.m..

The trolley bus fleet was only just coping with war time loads and spares for the Garrett buses were hard to come by. In February 1941 one of the buses, No 42 suddenly swerved when passing along Effingham Street and crashed into a house. It was admitted the accident was due to a steering defect. The bus was de-licensed and stood in the depot for some years. It was not repaired until the end of the war; it finally returned to service in May 1947 repainted in the new green livery. In April Conisbrough Council was pleased to note the Mexborough & Swinton Traction Co had agreed to their request that, between 1.30 and 2.30 p.m. certain buses should be reserved for work people only. It was not noted how the conductor was to decide who were work people, presumably a lady with a baby would be left. In September the company was censured by the Conisbrough Council for turning buses at the Dale instead of going all the way to Conanby, although the full fare to Conanby was being taken. There was trouble at the Conisbrough end with the trolley bus power supply due to an excessive voltage drop, causing particularly slow speeds when more than one vehicle was drawing power. To cope with this in June 1941 it was agreed to spend £900 on equipment to prevent the trouble and arrangements were made with the Yorkshire Electricity Power Company to provide the necessary supply. The alteration provided by a booster was only a palliative and there was to be further trouble at a later date.

Once again in February 1942, the Company had to apologise for the inconvenience to its passengers because several buses were not in use at peak times " owing to the sickness prevailing among their staff." In March, Mr McGibbon - for so many years manager of the Company and by now the managing director, tendered his resignation, which was accepted. He retained his seat on the board of directors until his death on 13 November 1945. During 1942 the company was able to purchase six old Guy six wheel single deck trolley buses from the Hastings Tramways Company at a cost of £1,050 the lot. They dated from 1928 and were similar to the Rotherham ones which had been purchased for the conversion of the Mexborough tramway to trolley bus operation; numbered 16, 29, 47, 48, 52 and 53 at Hastings they took the numbers of 70 – 75 in the Mexborough fleet. One record at Rawmarsh Road suggested that only three of these were used in service – whilst another archive suggests that No 75 was only used for spares. Certainly No 75 was sent for scrap in December 1945, some 6 months before any of the remainder, from July 1946 to July 1947.

No 3 (EWT 480), one of the six war time "utility" trolley buses in 1946 after its repaint from war time grey into the new green livery. There were detail differences between these and the post war additions. The front indicator had no section for the route letter, while with the registration plates higher on the front panel the curved green portion was flatter than in the later buses. The off front corner view is interesting in that on the roof to the right is the local air raid siren.

Two illustrations of the Hastings six wheel single deck trolley buses of 1928, six of which were purchased for use at Mexborough in 1942. Neither of these two were amongst those which went to Mexborough.

In 1943, the Company was fortunate in receiving six new "Utility" trolley buses. These came in two batches, the first three in March and the remainder a month later. They had 32 seat bodies by Brush, on Karrier trolley bus chassis - also referred to as a Sunbeam chassis. The query is still were they manufactured in the Karrier works in Huddersfield or at the Sunbeam works in Coventry?

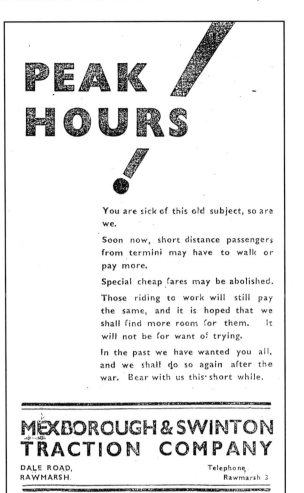

PEAK HOURS!

You are sick of this old subject, so are we.

Soon now, short distance passengers from termini may have to walk or pay more.

Special cheap fares may be abolished.

Those riding to work will still pay the same, and it is hoped that we shall find more room for them. It will not be for want of trying.

In the past we have wanted you all, and we shall do so again after the war. Bear with us this short while.

MEXBOROUGH & SWINTON TRACTION COMPANY

DALE ROAD, RAWMARSH.

Telephone, Rawmarsh 3

A wartime advertisement published in the Rotherham Express in May 1942. Definitely this was the shape of things to come!

Certainly the order in December 1941 for 6 trolley buses at £1,506 per chassis was with Sunbeam Commercial vehicles. The estimate for the bodies was a price of £1,000 each. In March 1942 it was decided to order a further nine trolley buses at an estimated cost of £2,600 each, but it was after the war before any more new trolley buses were received. It was noted in Modern Transport for August 1943 that the Mexborough & Swinton Traction Co had a new single deck Sunbeam trolley bus. They were provided with wartime wooden seating and painted in the prevailing wartime grey.

At Rotherham a single pair of trolley bus wires had been erected from a junction with the existing wiring by Grafton Bridge, running along Rawmarsh Road to join the Greasbrough route overhead at Chantry Bridge. From Sunday 20 September 1942, the Parkgate and Mexborough trolley buses were re - routed to use Rawmarsh Road continuing up Bridgegate to a terminal loop adjacent to All Saints Square. Buses turned down Bridgegate and followed the old route back to Grafton Bridge.

At what was one of the worst periods of the war, from the 3 November 1942, "ordinary" bus traffic ceased from 9.00 p.m.. An unusual purchase in the autumn of 1943 was a second hand 10 cwt Morris van from S. B. Hogg of Sheffield for £165. It was fitted with seats - not for bus service - but particularly for picking up road staff for early morning duties. There was much trouble with staff not turning up for duty at this period and presumably this innovation was to combat the tendency. The Company carried more and more passengers in spite of the aged vehicles, with vehicle mileage of 1,116,707 in 1939 they carried some 10,143,000 passengers. At the height of the war in 1942, with a maximum mileage of 1,203,872, they moved 15,350,000 passengers. As the war progressed, mileage declined slightly to 1,169,000 in 1944 with passengers now reducing to 14,884,000. In June 1945 it was decided to purchase 2 buses from Sheffield United Tours, not for passengers but as the basis for two tower wagons to replace the existing time expired units. The depot staff managed by "much initiative and ingenuity" to keep the fleet operational; by the war end some of the trolley buses had over 600,000 miles to their credit. Mr A E Davies, who followed Mr McGibbon as Engineer and Manager, retired at the end of 1946. A transport journal noted that he had been one of those managers who never appeared greatly in the limelight but he had been a great manager and had kept the fleet in a state of maintenance during the war years which did him infinite credit. Under him the undertaking had practically doubled the number of passengers carried annually. He was succeeded by Mr T P O'Donnell who joined the Company from a post with the London Transport Board. As he arrived it was noted that the British Thomson Houston Co had an order for 12 trolley bus equipment's for the Mexborough & Swinton Traction Co .

The Ministry of Transport had refused to issue a permit to purchase the 9 trolley buses which the Company wished to order in 1942, now the directors decided to apply for a licence to order 3 more trolley buses and to press the Ministry to authorise the purchase of 12 trolley buses. On 30 June 1945, the Company were at last given an allocation to purchase 10 buses plus an additional allocation for a further 8. The cost was estimated at £1,700 per chassis and £1,100 for the bodies. An order for 12 more Sunbeam Trolley buses was passed in May 1946

A near side view of No 8 (FWX 892) when just delivered in 1947

No 8 (FWX 892 - The interior looking forward.

the cost now being estimated at £3,200 each. The first batch of 18, delivered in 1947 were fitted with BTH 207A3, 85 HP motors. The following 12 which arrived in 1948 had 95 HP motors, BTH type 207A73. All of them had 32 seat Brush single deck centre entrance bodies. The original Garrett trolley bus fleet was already long past its sell by date, in the year ended December 21 1945 three, numbers 34, 37 and 38 were sold for scrap along with No 75 of the ex - Hastings Guys which had never been used in service by the Mexborough company. Additionally, the old petrol engined Albion, No 91, which had been new to Hebble in 1928, was also disposed of. Three more trolley buses, a Garrett, No 49, and two of the Guys Nos. 70 & 74 went in 1946. The new Sunbeam/Brush trolley buses delivered in 1947 and 1948 were painted, not in the old Mexborough dark red but in a livery of green, which became the new standard fleet colour. With their arrival further old trolley buses went to scrap. Between May and August 1947, the last of the Guys went to the breakers along with a dozen of the Garretts, and also No 68 one of the ex Notts. and Derby buses. Incidentally, two of the first Garretts to go in May 1947 were from the last batch of three which had been built in 1930, while the last of

these went in July. When all of the new fleet were delivered 36 new Sunbeams replaced 32 Garretts and the six ex Notts. and Derby trolley buses. As replacements for the old petrol buses, three Bedford OB's with Duple bodies were received in 1948 along with another second hand from the East Yorkshire Co fleet. In May 1947 while large numbers of the old trolley buses were being scrapped, the directors asked the manager to make a report on what would be the maximum numbers of trolley buses needed to provide an adequate service. He reported that they could cope with a fleet of 33 new Sunbeam when in service but finally it was decided in January 1949 to buy a further 3 Sunbeam trolley buses. They arrived in August 1950, Nos. 37 to 39 (SWW 375/7) with similar equipment to their immediate predecessors. They were to prove to be the last new trolley buses to join the fleet. A spare motor to serve the new fleet was purchased in 1948 at a cost of £300, while the original wartime Sunbeams were provided with heaters. It was noted that the 12 trolley vehicles had cost £8,295 over the estimate.

Operating costs continued to rise in the years after the war ended, with almost annual general wage increases. In 1946 the company decided that fare increases on the trolley bus section were needed to keep the company "out of the red". Accordingly, using its rights under the Act to fix fares within the statutory limits, they increased the fares from September 23rd. The local Councils concerned, Rawmarsh, Swinton, Mexborough and Conisbrough joined in condemnation of the increases and protested to the Ministry of Transport which decided to hold a public enquiry and arranged for it to take place in the Sheffield Town Hall on January 30 1947. Mr Eastwood, Chairman of the Yorkshire traffic area conducted the inquiry. Sir Edwin Herbert on behalf of the Company explained that the minimum fare had been increased from one penny to three half pence and the 12 journey ticket had been increased "in line" with the ordinary fare increase. Neither the main body of the ordinary fares nor the workmen's fares had been altered. He pointed out that the 12 journey ticket was not required under the Companies Acts and had been introduced "entirely at the company's volition". The Company had found the ticket open to abuse and had been surprised to find under the new system how much this ticket had been abused. It was felt that, without the increase the Company would not pay a dividend in 1947. The manager admitted that some fare stages had been altered and some anomalies had arisen which had been amended already. Mr Eastwood in summing up noted that because of the stage changes, some fares, such as between

Station Hotel and Brook Square had been increased by 100% - this section being one of the best paying portions of the whole route. He objected to the anomalies - in one case of a 3d stage the third stage only went 100 yards for a penny while it cost an extra $\frac{1}{2}$d to travel between two stops in Mexborough High Street.

Sir Edwin Herbert protested that the fares had been fixed within the maximum allowed by its Acts. He concluded "Let no one go away from this inquiry thinking that this is a well to do company wanting to increase fares deliberately. Our expenses have gone up but our fares have not although our travellers have received large increases in remuneration during war time." The Company's expenditure had risen from £36,607 in 1937 to £67,252 in 1945 but fares had been practically unchanged from 1929. At the end the local councils had the offer that they could negotiate with the company on the points raised - but Mr Drabble appearing for the Councils wished the Minister to make the decision. When this was received, the councils claimed "victory" - penny fares were reintroduced while as an example a new 2/-d weekly ticket from Adwick Road junction to Woodman had been issued over the ordinary 3d stage.

The Company was still showing interest in extending their system into areas not yet reached. New housing was being built at Windhill, some half mile further along the road from the Mexborough (Adwick Road) terminus. The very narrow lane at Conisbrough on the way to Conanby (Conisbrough High) had always been the cause of trouble and it was decided to build a separate route here by way of Station Road to give one way traffic over the section with "down" buses using the old route and "up" the new way.

A rear view of Bus No 80 (EBT 240) standing at the Greasbrough Terminus, this bus, a Bedford OB with a Roe 30 seat body, started life in 1946 with G Crosby of Normanby. It passed in November 1947 to the East Yorkshire Co who sold it to the Mexborough & Swinton Traction Co in January 1948.

Two official notices

1) The authority to proceed with the trolley bus extensions November 1946

2) The later Provisional Order permitting the extensions May 1947

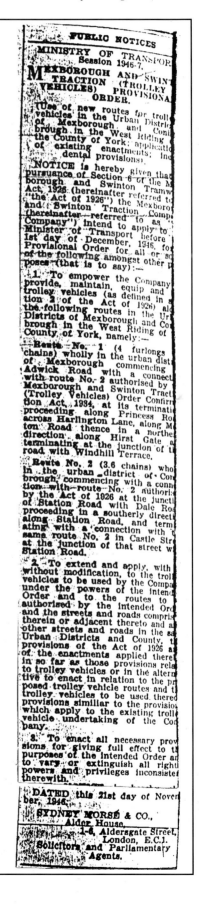

AUGUST 24, 1946

THE MEXBOROUGH AND SWINTON TRACTION COMPANY.

NOTICE

Owing to the large increases in wages, and the rapidly rising cost of all materials, the Company has reluctantly been compelled to revise the fare list. These revisions take the form of abolition of the 1d. fare, with one exception, and increases in the cost of 12 journey tickets. At the same time, the opportunity has been taken to remove anomalies from the existing fare list. These alterations will come into operation on 23rd September, 1946. A copy of the complete amended fare list is displayed in this vehicle.

12 JOURNEY TICKETS

Whilst there has been abuse by some members of the public in the use of the present 12 journey ticket, the Company has no desire to withdraw the facility which this type of ticket offers to regular travellers, but will alter the conditions of issue in order to prevent further abuse. In consequence—

(1) 12 journey tickets in their present form will not be valid after Sunday, 22nd September, 1946.

(2) 12 journey tickets will be issued for a further period with conditions of issue as follows:—

As from Monday, 23rd September, 1946—
Period of availability to be 7 days from Monday to the following Sunday inclusive, after which period the ticket will be invalid.

Available for workpeople only, when travelling to and from their work, and only for journeys between the stage points punched on the ticket.

6 outward journeys (from the direction of Rotherham) and 6 inward journeys (towards Rotherham) may be taken.

No rebate will be allowed for the non-use of this ticket to its full extent.

Not transferable.

Subject to the Bye-laws and Regulations of the Company

The Mexborough and Swinton Traction Company.

LIST OF FARES

Stage No.																	
1..	Rotherham																
2..	1	Rotherham Bridge															
3..	2	1½	Midland Street														
4..	2	1½	1½	Hollybush Street													
5..	3	2	1½	1½	Rawmarsh Post Office												
6..	4	3	3	2	1½	Kilnhurst Road											
7..	4	4	3	3	2	1½	Wentworth Road										
8..	5	4	4	3	3	2	1½	Woodman's Inn									
9..	5	5	4	4	3	3	1½	1½	Milton Street or Manvers Main								
10..	6	5	5	4	4	3	2	1½	1½	Swinton Station or Highwoods Road							
11..	6	6	5	5	4	4	3	2	1½	1½	City Bank						
12..	7	6	6	5	5	4	4	3	2	1½	1½	Adwick Road Junction					
13A	7	7	6	6	5	5	4	4	3	2	1½	1½	Old Toll Bar or Adwick Road Terminus				
14..	8	7	7	6	6	5	5	4	4	3	2	1½	1½	Denaby Pit			
15..	8	8	7	7	6	6	5	5	4	4	3	2	1½	1½	Denaby Main Hotel		
16..	9	8	8	7	7	6	9	5	5	4	4	3	2	2	1½	Burcroft or Conisbro Co-op	
17..	9	9	8	8	7	7	6	6	5	5	4	4	3	3	2	1½	Brooke Square or Conanby.

WORKPEOPLE'S 12 JOURNEY TICKETS.

1/6

Rotherham Bridge	To	Rawmarsh P.O.
Hollybush Street	,,	Kilnhurst Road
Rawmarsh Post Off.	,,	Wentworth Road
Kilnhurst Road	,,	Woodman's Inn
Wentworth Road	,,	Swinton Station
Woodman's Inn	,,	City Bank
Milton Street	,,	Adwick Rd. Junctn.
Manvers Main	,,	Adwick Rd. Junctn.
Swinton Station	,,	Old Toll Bar
Swinton Station	,,	Adwick Rd. Ter.
Highwoods Road	,,	Old Toll Bar
City Bank	,,	Denaby Pit
Adwick Rd. Junctn.	,,	Denaby Main Hotel
Old Toll Bar	,,	Burcroft
Old Toll Bar	,,	Conisbro' Co-op.
Denaby Pit	,,	Brooke Square
Cadeby Pit	,,	Conanby

2/-

Rotherham Bridge	To	Kilnhurst Road
Midland Street	,,	Wentworth Road
Hollybush Street	,,	Woodman's Inn
Rawmarsh Post Off.	,,	Milton Street
Kilnhurst Road	,,	Swinton Station
Wentworth Road	,,	City Bank
Woodman's Inn	,,	Adwick Rd Junctn.
Milton Street	,,	Old Toll Bar
Milton Street	,,	Adwick Rd. Junctn.
Manvers Main	,,	Old Toll Bar
Swinton Station	,,	Denaby Pit
Highwoods Road	,,	Denaby Pit
City Bank	,,	Cadeby Pit
Adwick Rd. Junctn.	,,	Burcroft
Adwick Rd. Junctn.	,,	Conisbro' Co-op.
Old Toll Bar	,,	Brooke Square
Denaby Pit	,,	Conanby

Period of availability to be 7 days from MONDAY to the following SUNDAY inclusive, after which period the Ticket WILL BE INVALID; available for Workpeople only, when travelling to and from their work, and only for journeys between the Stage Points punched on the Ticket. 6 Outward Journeys (From Rotherham) and 6 Inward Journeys (Towards Rotherham) may be taken. No rebate will be allowed for the non-use of this ticket to its full extent. Not transferable. Subject to the Bye-Laws and Regulations of the Company.

WORKMEN'S TICKETS—Issued before 8 a.m. and after 5 p.m. Daily, Saturdays 12 noon to 2 p.m. (Sundays and Public Holidays excepted), at undermentioned rates:—

CHILDREN'S FARES—Children under 3 years of age are allowed to travel Free; above 3 but under 14 years of age will be charged at undermentioned rates:—

Where Ordinary Fare is ..	1½d.	2d.	3d.	4d.	5d.	6d.	7d.	8d.	9d.
Workmen's Fare is ..	1d.	1½d.	2d.	3d.	4d.	5d.	6d.	7d.	8d.
Children's Fare is	1d.	1d.	2d.	2d.	3d.	3d.	4d.	4d.	5d.

September, 1946.

By Order,
A. A. DAVIS, Managing Engineer,
Dale Road, Rawmarsh.

For this change the Ministry of Transport issued a special order in May 1947 allowing the Company to make the alteration prior to the confirming Bill, to cover the work, passing through Parliament. The alteration was taken in hand as soon as possible and the new section was opened on 12 April 1948. In the Bill the Company were empowered to extend the route from Adwick Road for half a mile into the Windhill Estate.

This addition had first been proposed in 1937 when it had been estimated that it would cost £800. In November 1946 it was decided to proceed with the extension - now estimated to cost £1,550 while the cost of the necessary Provisional Order would add a further £200. The new estimate was far from accurate. In September 1949, after enquiry, the best offer for building the half mile was some £3,424 so it was decided to invite competitive tenders. No firm tendered and it was decided not to proceed with the extension for the time being.

By September 1947 with 24 of the replacement trolley buses in service, it was felt that it was possible to slightly "speed up" the timing on the main line from Conisbrough and Adwick road to Rotherham. The new buses were a little higher powered than their predecessors while work at Bridgegate in Rotherham permitted a time saving of some 3 minutes. To give a 7 1/2 minute headway between Mexborough and Rotherham, trolley buses on the Adwick road section were allowed a ten minute layover to fit in. This was now reduced to only 2 minutes while a minute was cut from the running time - presumably one bus less would be needed. Passengers were asked to give clear signals to the drivers at stops.

With the construction of the one way system at Conisbrough, the Company, with the full support of the Councils, requested the Ministry to allow the use of buses of the newly permitted 8 ft width in replacement of their 7' 6" vehicles. Before the change to the new one way street operation the local police had objected to the change on the ground that the narrow place, only 200 yards in length, would be too dangerous to accommodate 8 ft wide buses. With the alterations both Company and Council felt that the improvement had made the way clear. They were very disappointed when the Ministry refused the Application. On June 7 the local paper in a leading article noted that "Passengers who have been subjected to rush hour crushing during the hot weather will be extremely disappointed to learn that the application of the Company for permission to operate 8 ft wide buses has been turned down. The larger size does not increase the carrying capacity of the buses but greatly enhances their comfort. The Ministry of Transport have offered no reason for their refusal and their arbitrary attitude is not calculated to make the veto go down any better among those denied what seems a very reasonable easement of public transport conditions." With the gradual post war decline in the number of passengers being carried, it was decided that whilst it was now possible to make the change, the additional turning circle at Kilnhurst Road was no longer needed. Therefore in 1948 the manager's authority to spend £110, the 1940 cost figure, was rescinded. Already extensions of the trolley bus system were becoming subject to doubts. In January 1950, with the formation of the new Electricity Board and the demise of the Rotherham and Mexborough local ownership, the Mexborough company found it necessary to purchase the substations at Rawmarsh and Swinton from the new Board. That at Swinton cost nearly £3,000 and the Rawmarsh one £1,500. Rotherham Corporation agreed to sell their rectifier and plant to the Company for £2,250, but this had to be re-sited to be of use as a Company supply point. The additional plant needed at Rawmarsh substation cost £128 and that at Swinton £483. The Company were able to purchase 44 second hand poles and four tons of trolley wire from the Gateshead and District Tramway Company at a cost of £2,500 during September 1950.

In 1947 when the Windhill trolley bus extension was being considered, enquiries as to suppliers of materials produced the information that, if ordered at once, there was no chance of delivery before the spring of 1950. It was also noted that the power supply position between Mexborough and Conisbrough was such that for the extension, a new substation was needed. It would seem that it was needed in any case, since the proposed half mile extra from Adwick Road would not have unduly increased demand. The new manager had decided that the whole of the overhead equipment needed large scale repairs, while he reported in February 1948 that improvements were needed in the electricity supply. It was agreed to spend £10,000 on new equipment. In view of this it was decided for the time being to provide a petrol bus service between Mexborough Railway Station and Windhill. When authorising the new route, the Traffic Commissioners were doubtful as to its prospects - and included a proviso that, after 8 weeks operation, the Company should report the results to date - to decide if it was worth continuing with the operation. The service, which commenced on Wednesday December 1st was half hourly. The route from the station was along Station Road to Bank Street where it followed the trolley bus

route to the Adwick Road terminus. It continued along Adwick Road, Princess Road and Morton Road into Hirst Gate to a terminus at Windhill Terrace. In January 1949 the Company manager made a proposal to the Mexborough Council for an extension of this route through Mexborough to the Don Hotel at Swinton, with a diversion at Mexborough along Jail Hill, cutting out the Station Road section. The Council were not happy about the Jail Hill proposal and referred the proposals to the next meeting of the Transport Committee to report back on the alterations.

On the 31 January 1949 the "booster" for the power on the Conisbrough section failed. The sections could still be operated for normal service - but any overload had to be avoided. To cope with the situation a weekday petrol bus shuttle service between the Old Toll Bar and Brook Square was introduced - the Conisbrough High route was maintained. It is noted that Rotherham's very high powered buses occasionally ran to Brook Square and they would certainly have affected the load. However, passengers disliking the change at the Old Toll bar used the "High" trolley buses as much as possible and finally it was decided to put on normal service and "hope for the best". When introducing the shuttle service it was thought that it would be the year end before the new equipment was installed. It had been decided to provide a new rectifier substation and not attempt to repair the "booster".

A diesel bus travelling up one of the narrow Conisbrough streets "under the wire" which was soon to go. Bus No 54 (WWW 54), on its way to Conanby, was new in 1959, one of the buses which would replace the trolley buses. *Courtesy D Dodd.*

It has been suggested that at this time Sheffield Corporation had a mercury arc rectifier on order for use on the proposed extension of the Wadsley Bridge tramway which finally did not take place, and that the

Mexborough & Swinton Traction Co took over the order. Certainly the Company were able to report by September that they would soon be able to provide an improved service to Conisbrough High, which was much sooner than had been expected in February. A new substation was being built on a piece of land adjoining the North Eastern division Coal Board's Area Headquarters at Conisbrough. This was provided with a 750 kW rectifier which would provide ample power for the whole of the Conisbrough area trolley vehicle services. The new substation was brought into operation on 15 September 1949. On Saturday October 8th the Company announced that from the following Monday an increased service of a bus every 8 minutes instead of ten minute intervals at peak hours, so that in a two hour period there would be 17 buses on the Manvers - Conisbrough High route instead of up to 12 at that time. They also intended to give a better service at some other periods.

The manager began to complain to the road authorities about the too frequent flooding of Rowms Lane after the Rotherham service was twice halted in 3 days in October. He pointed out that to run the trolley buses with the motors in water was liable to incur a cost of £200 for a rewind. He had the support of the local councils concerned, since they were already asking the District Council to "do something about it".

Costs were continually rising and by 1950 the auxiliary petrol bus services had been loss makers for some years, the final "blow" being the increase in fuel tax of May 1950. This alteration alone increased the loss on the buses by some £265 per annum. In the circumstances an application was made for fare increases on the bus services. The Commissioners heard the application at a sitting in Rotherham on 19 December 1950. The petrol bus services were then from Low Stubbin to Kilnhurst, Greasbrough to Kilnhurst and Rosehill Park to Kilnhurst Colliery. The application was granted and the new fares came into operation from Monday January 29th 1951. The concession return fares between Sandhill, Rawmarsh and Kilnhurst, together with special children's fare were abolished, whilst colliery workers weekly tickets were replaced by daily workmen's return tickets. The ordinary fare table maintained the penny fares, except where the buses were operating over the trolley bus routes. It was

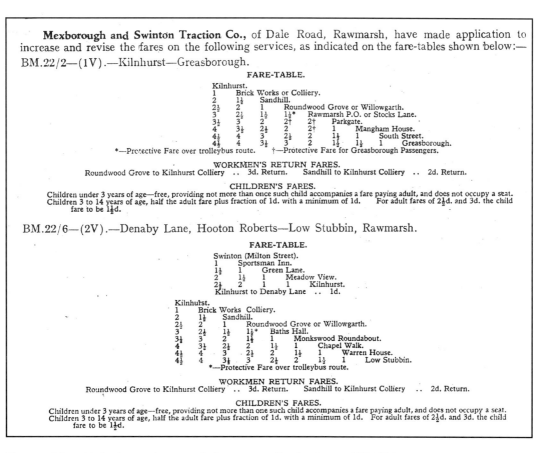

The revised fare table for the petrol services which came into effect from January 25th 1951.

BURROWS'
MOTOR COACH SERVICES

RAWMARSH
Parkgate
Greasboro'
Wentworth
Wath
WOMBWELL
Barnsley
Wakefield
LEEDS

A BURROWS
" JUBILEE "

Started With Wagonette—
Now Nearly 100 Employees
ROMANCE OF
WOMBWELL
UNDERTAKING

LEEDS
Wakefield
Barnsley
Wombwell
WATH
Wentworth
Greasboro'
Parkgate
RAWMARSH

Excursions and Tours Start from the New Market Place.

BOOK YOUR COACHES FOR PRIVATE PARTIES.

We invite your inspection of our Luxury Coaches

Wombwell to Pontefract	Wombwell to Doncaster Parkgate to Doncaster	Wombwell to Sheffield
Race Meetings Only.	Race Meetings Only.	Football and Cricket Matches Only.

TAXIS FOR HIRE !

Further Particulars : Apply T. Burrows & Sons, Jubilee Garage, Wombwell.
PHONE WOMBWELL 2383

RAWMARSH—LEEDS

		WEEKDAYS								Sundays
		a.m.	a.m.	a.m.	a.m.	p.m.	p.m.	p.m.	p.m.	a.m.
RAWMARSH (Baths Hall) .. dep.		—	—	6.30	7.30	7.30	8.30	9.30	10.30	8.30
Parkgate (Fitzwilliam Arms H'l) „		—	6.0	6.35	7.35	7.35	8.35	9.35	10.35	8.35
Greasborough (Church Street) „		—	6.7	6.42	7.42	7.42	8.42	9.42	10.42	8.40
Wentworth (Church) .. „		—	—	6.52	7.52	7.52	8.52	9.52	10.52	8.52
Brampton (Church) .. „		5.5	6.5	7.5	8.5	8.5	9.5	10.5	11.5	9.5
Wath & West Melton (Police S.) „		5.7	6.7	7.7	8.7	8.7	9.7	10.7	11.7	9.7
Wombwell (Church) .. „		5.15	6.15	7.15	8.15	8.15	9.15	10.15	11.15	9.15
Stairfoot (Bull Hotel) .. „		5.25	6.25	7.25	8.25	8.25	9.25	—	—	9.25
BARNSLEY (Bus Station) .. „		5.35	6.35	7.35	8.35	8.35	9.35	To Wombwell		9.35
Staincross (Four Lane Ends) „		5.48	6.48	7.48	8.48	8.48	—	only		9.48
Newmillerdam (Fox & Hounds) „		6.0	7.0	8.0	9.0	9.0	—			10.0
WAKEFIELD (Wood Street) .. „		6.20	7.20	8.20	9.20	9.20	—			10.20
Stanley (Railway Station) .. „		6.33	7.33	8.33	9.33	9.33	—			10.33
... „		6.41	7.41	8.41	9.41	9.41	—			10.41
Thwaite Gate .. „		6.50	7.50	8.50	9.50	9.50	—			10.50
LEEDS (St. Peter's Bus Stn.) .. arr.		7.0	8.0	9.0	10.0	10.0	—			11.0

		WEEKDAYS								Sundays
		a.m.	a.m.	a.m.	a.m.	p.m.	p.m.	p.m.	p.m.	a.m.
LEEDS (St. Peter's Bus Stn.) .. dep.		—	—	—	7.5	8.5	—	9.5	10.5	11.5
Thwaite Gate .. „		—	—	—	7.14	8.14	—	9.14	10.14	11.14
Oulton (Lodge) .. „		—	—	—	7.23	8.23	—	9.23	10.23	11.23
Stanley (Railway Station) .. „		—	—	—	7.31	8.31	—	9.31	10.31	11.31
WAKEFIELD (Springs) .. „		—	—	—	7.45	8.45	—	9.45	10.45	11.45
Newmillerdam Dam Inn .. „		—	—	—	8.0	9.0	—	10.0	11.0	12.0
Staincross (Four Lane Ends) .. „		—	—	7.12	8.12	9.12	—	10.12	11.12	12.12
BARNSLEY Bus Station) .. „		—	—	7.25	8.25	9.25	9.40	10.25	11.25	12.25
Stairfoot (Bull Hotel) .. „		—	—	7.33	8.31	9.33	9.47	10.33	11.33	12.33
Wombwell (Church) .. „		4.45	5.45	6.42	7.42	8.42	9.42	9.56	10.42	11.42	a.m. 7.42	12.42
Wath & West Melton Police S.) „		5.0	5.52	6.49	7.49	8.49	—	9.49	10.2	10.49	—	7.49	12.49
Brampton Church) .. „		5.2	5.54	6.51	7.51	8.51	—	9.51	10.5	10.51	—	7.51	12.51
Wentworth Church .. „		5.14	—	7.3	8.3	9.3	—	10.3	—	—	—	8.3	1.3
Greasborough (Prince of Wales) „		5.40	6.12	7.13	8.13	9.13	—	10.13	—	—	—	8.13	1.13
Parkgate (Fitzwilliam Arms H'l) „		5.47	6.20	7.18	8.18	9.18	—	10.18	—	—	—	8.14	1.18
RAWMARSH Baths Hall arr.		—	—	7.25	8.25	9.25	—	10.25	—	—	—	8.25	1.25

Weekdays : Early Morning Run—Fitzwilliam Arms Hotel, Parkgate a.47 a.m.
Aldwarke Main Colliery 6.0 a.m. to Parkgate.

CUT THIS TIMETABLE OUT—YOU MAY NEED IT.

Burrows "Jubilee" advertisement in April 1950.

No 53 (EVG 26) one of Burrows buses standing in Barnsley on its journey from Leeds to Rawmarsh. *Photo courtesy D Dodd*

The low railway bridge on the route from Mexborough to Manvers Main, which was too low to allow double deck buses to pass.

DONCASTER — CONANBY SERVICE

Operated jointly by Doncaster, Rotherham and Sheffield Transport Departments.

TRAFFIC NOTICE

SUNDAY TIME TABLE

Commencing **SUNDAY, 25th NOVEMBER, 1951**, and continuing until further notice, a service between **DONCASTER** and **CONANBY** will be instituted and will operate at the following times:-

	p.m.	p.m.	p.m.	p.m.	p.m.	p.m.	p.m.	p.m.	p.m.	p.m.
DONCASTER, Glasgow Paddocks Dept:	1.00	2.00	3.00	4.00	5.00	6.00	7.00	8.00	9.00	10.05
CONANBY, St. Andrew's Mission Arr:	1.25	2.25	3.25	4.25	5.25	6.25	7.25	8.25	9.25	10.28
CONANBY, St. Andrew's Mission Dept:	1.30	2.30	3.30	4.30	5.30	6.30	7.30	8.30	9.30	10.30
DONCASTER, Glasgow Paddocks Arr:	1.55	2.55	3.55	4.55	5.55	6.55	7.55	8.55	9.55	10.55

Transport Offices,
Leicester Avenue,
Doncaster.
19/11/1951.

T. POTTS,
General Manager.

R. L. CROWTHER, PRINTER, SUNNY BAR, DONCASTER

Doncaster Corporation was interested in the Conanby end of the Mexborough operations

anticipated that the charges would give a revenue increase of some £400 per annum. The Company also gave notice that a general fare increase over the trolley vehicle routes was imminent.

In October 1950 at a meeting of the Rotherham Rural District Council, the Councillor representing the Brampton district referred to the lack of a direct bus service from there to Rotherham. Burrows and Sons of Wombwell were interested in this request since their Rawmarsh to Leeds service covered most of this route. Between Rawmarsh and Wath upon Dearne this was by way of Parkgate, Greasbrough, Wentworth and

Brampton. He had applied in July 1946 for a licence to operate a service from Wombwell to Rotherham by way of the long gone D.D.L.R tram route to Woodman Inn and thence along the trolley bus route to Rotherham. This had been opposed, not only by the local bus companies, but also by the Rotherham R.D.C. and had been refused. Burrows was one of the early South Yorkshire bus operators, who had commenced operations in 1909 when he started a Saturday horse waggonette service between Wombwell and Darfield. In 1914 with his first petrol engined vehicle, a Belsize with an 8 seat body, he started a service from West Melton to Barnsley. Once the war was over the firm began to expand, purchasing a 28 seat Daimler charabanc (C 2895) in 1921 followed by a 26 seat Vulcan "saloon coach" (WT 637) in 1923. On April 6 1925 they extended their route to run from Wath upon Dearne, through Wombwell and Barnsley to Leeds. The original service ran three times a day. In 1930, they again extended the route to start at Rawmarsh Baths and by 1950 an hourly service was given between Rawmarsh and Leeds.

After the request by the Rotherham R.D.C. for a service from Brampton direct to Rotherham, Burrows applied to the Traffic Commissioners for a licence for the route, passing through the new Rawmarsh, Monkwood Estate to Parkgate and Rotherham. They were gladly supported in the application by Rawmarsh Council who were already wanting a service to the new estate and the direct connection to Rotherham satisfied their need. However, the Traffic Commissioners, in their wisdom, rejected the application and for the time being only the trolley buses connected Rawmarsh with Rotherham.

The Yorkshire Traction Co Ltd management announced at the beginning of 1951 that they intended to introduce low bridge double deck buses on the Barnsley, Mexborough, Doncaster route. To allow for this the route between Wath upon Dearne and Mexborough had to be changed since only single deck buses could pass under the low railway bridge near to Manvers on the straight road from Wath upon Dearne. By the altered route the buses were now to travel from Wath upon Dearne up Burman Road to the Mexborough & Swinton trolley bus route which would be followed as far as Mexborough. Under its Act the Mexborough & Swinton Traction Co could claim preferential fares over this section but their right to this benefit was waived and the Yorkshire Traction fares were the same as the Mexborough & Swinton Company fares. The two companies were gradually drawing closer to each other. The new service started on Saturday 20 January and the passengers let the single deck buses pass in order to ride on the new double deckers. There was an illustration showing Yorkshire Traction bus No 937, (DHE 574) passing under the Swinton railway bridge - the trolley bus wiring appeared to be very close to the bus roof but there never seems to have been a report of a contact.

To cover the loss of the old route, the existing Yorkshire Traction route from the New Hill Estate, Wath upon Dearne to Mexborough which had terminated at Grange road was extended to the top of Cemetery Road then along New Hall Road to the Crown Inn and from there along Grange Road to follow the normal route.

Swinton Council now decided to meet the Mexborough & Swinton manager with a request for a "circular" bus service from Manvers Main Colliery via Bolton Road to the new Highfield Farm Estate and Bow Broom. They discussed a number of possible routes but hoped that one could be arranged which would justify full day operation. At the same time they pointed out that, as a priority, they were still waiting for a circular service for the Piccadilly residents.

Across the River Don opposite Mexborough there is the village of Old Denaby. There was a penny ferry across the river, but to reach the Mexborough shops by road, the Old Denaby residents had to walk beside the river as far as Denaby before being able to cross the river by Pastures Bridge. They had been asking for a footbridge - without success - for years. Now the 150 village residents decided to ask the two companies, Yorkshire Traction and Mexborough & Swinton for a bus service at least on Mondays and Saturdays from 10.00 am to 2.00 p.m. with a late bus on Saturday "so that they could go to the cinema once a week". Neither company showed the slightest interest.

The local councils now began to "lean" on the Mexborough Company; in March 1951, Mexborough Council objected to a Mexborough & Swinton Traction Co proposed variation to the Windhill Estate service. The bus route was not paying and in spite of the Council's objection, the Company was authorised in April to convert the route to a one man operation to reduce costs. At this date, the Company had not yet taken any Diesel engined buses into the fleet - probably one or two of the Bedford OB's were adjusted to allow for driver fare collection.

The fare increase on the trolley bus route came into effect from Monday June 4 1951. The changes were in some things similar to the January petrol bus fare alterations but, as compared with the short ancillary services, the change affected the whole district. The special fare between Rotherham and the Parkgate Iron and Steel Works which had cost 1/6d for the week, was abolished. Ordinary fares rose from 2d to 2 1/2d and 3 1/2d to 4d, while workmen's fares, only issued before 8.00 am were to be definitely for " artisans, mechanics and daily labourers with a minimum return fare of 3d for up to three stages. Returns were available at any hour of the day, Saturdays and Sundays excepted.

In June 1951 Rawmarsh Council decided that they wanted a meeting as soon as possible with Mr O'Donnell to discuss the fare increases. Mexborough Council were unhappy about the 8.00 am dead line for workmen's tickets since in the area many people worked shifts which could start at practically any hour of the day. The Councils had no success with the Company - whose manager pointed out that all the alterations were within the limits allowed under their Acts. On the operational side, 1951 was not a good year for the Company. In May trolley bus No 29 (FWX 913) suddenly swerved when travelling through Swinton and smashed into one of the standards which, though bent, took the strain. The front of No 29 was badly damaged and repairs must have been very expensive. In August the driver was summoned for dangerous driving - he did not know why the bus swerved but was fortunate to have the case dismissed. At the beginning of September after heavy rainfall, Rowms Lane was - as usual - flooded and services stopped for some hours from 6.30 in the evening. On 21 September there was a power failure to the trolley bus route which stopped all services from Mexborough to Conisbrough High and Brook Square for over an hour just on the evening peak. It was about this time in 1951 that Rotherham Corporation sold the rectifying equipment from the Fullerton Road substation to the Company.

In December 1951 Wath upon Dearne Council agreed to send a representative to a conference suggested by Mexborough Council for a joint discussion by them all of further imminent fare increases. On January 24 1952 at the meeting representatives from six local councils, Rawmarsh, Swinton, Mexborough, Conisbrough, Wath upon Dearne and Dearne decided that as soon as the Company made any application for a fare increase, they would hold a further meeting and, if necessary would engage counsel on their behalf - the cost to be covered by all six in proportion to their rateable value. On February 2nd the Company published its notice for fare increases on both trolley and petrol bus routes. The inquiry by the Ministry into the proposed increases was held in Rotherham on Tuesday 24 February 1952. For the Company it was claimed that without the increases they would be some £16,000 short of their requirements and that the proposed increase would produce about £18,700 for the year. They noted that new trolley buses were costing £4,900 each. It was proposed to increase the fares by ½d up to 5 stages and by 1d for above that. The Chairman decided that he needed more information and adjourned the inquiry to Monday April 21 when it was held at Wath upon Dearne Town Hall. For the Councils it was stated that since 1947 there had already been three fare increases and that during the period the company

had maintained a 10% dividend. In the last financial year the Company had carried forward the sum of £18,000. Their counsel, Mr Goss, suggested that if for once the Company reduced the dividend considerably, this sum would obviate the need for any increase for the year. The Company's counsel pointed out that a 10% dividend only cost £10,548 a year. During the past years the Company had ploughed back into the undertaking £195,000. Presumably this figure included the cost of the new trolley bus fleet, which alone must have cost at least £170,000. It was noted that the cost of new overhead equipment had increased by 20% "last month" which would add £460 to the annual bill. It is a fact that throughout the decade since the war ended, the cost of operating trolley buses rose considerably more than that for the contemporary diesel bus. Another factor was the cost of electricity which also rose disproportionately to bus fuel costs whilst some of the original equipment was now obsolete. In July 1952 it was agreed to replace the old Brown Bouverie steel tank rectifier, probably at Rawmarsh depot, with a new Hewittick rectifier at a cost of £2,250. There was a further meeting in Rotherham before Major Eastwood, Chairman of the Yorkshire Traffic Area on Wednesday 10 September 1952 when it was finally agreed that they would permit a fare increase of ½d up to 5 stages and 1d on six stages or more. The increase came into force from September 22.

July of 1952 produced more than the usual crop of trouble for the ageing trolley bus equipment. On the 1st there was a violent thunderstorm in the evening when two inches of rain fell over the district; in five places between Rotherham and Conisbrough the floods were such that the trolley buses could not be operated for the rest of the day. To add to the trouble, the Rawmarsh substation was struck by lightning while at Conisbrough and Mexborough the overhead wiring was damaged by lightning. The staff worked all night to repair the damage and by next morning they were able to give the normal service. Buses were provided to give a skeleton service on Tuesday night. Not improbably due to the storm effects, the wiring came down at a point between Conisbrough and Denaby a few weeks later, producing some interesting fireworks. Only the lines towards Denaby were down and after half an hour service was able to continue by swinging trolleys on to the other wires until repairs had been completed.

The petrol bus routes were still not proving profitable and on 23 February the Greasbrough to Parkgate service was withdrawn. It was replaced at the better paying end of the route by improving the service on the Parkgate via Rawmarsh to Kilnhurst section. The bus fleet changed in 1950 by the acquisition of Nos. 83 and 84, two Leyland's with Duple bodies from Sheffield United Tours. These, AWA 331 and AWA 332, had been fitted in 1934 with new chassis. In 1952 they were joined by the first diesel engined buses in the fleet, numbered 85 to 88 (DDV 447, 441, 442 and 451 respectively). They were new to Devon General in 1939, AEC Regals with 35 seat front entrance Harrington bodies. They entered the Mexborough & Swinton Traction Co fleet between May and July. The post war Bedfords were also reaching the end of their life at Mexborough; in May 1952 it was decided to scrap No 80 which was out of use with an engine "beyond repair". The ex - Devon General buses only cost £200 each. With their arrival it was agreed to scrap three more Bedfords, Nos. 77 - 79. However in September they were sold to Sheffield United Tours for £110 each. It was not until November 1953 that No 82, the last of the Bedfords, was disposed of, sold for £150 "for use abroad" - its final destination is not known. During this period the Windhill Route, having proved completely loss making, was withdrawn on 30 June 1953.

The condition of the trolley vehicle equipment was still causing concern to such an extent that, in 1952 it was realised that the overhead equipment on the Green Lane section would have to be completely renewed. Finally in March 1953 it was decided to convert the route to diesel bus operation, even though this would involve the disposal of some 6 trolley buses which, though the chassis still had a long life, the bodies were already worn out and due for replacement. Six large capacity diesel engined single deck buses would be needed, to cost £4,000 each, whilst it was felt on the remaining trolley bus installation two new reversing points would be needed. One at Hawley Street, Rawmarsh and the other at Romwood Avenue, Swinton. In May orders were placed for six Leyland Tiger Cubs with MCW bodies and four more to replace the second hand ex Devon General buses. It was not until September 1953 that the Company officially informed Rotherham Corporation that they wished to apply for licences to operate public service vehicles (buses) over the whole of the joint trolley vehicle services. In September accordingly, the Corporation decided to give the Company the statutory six months notice to terminate the agreement with the Company. In November the Company applied to the Traffic

Scenes on the Mexborough trolley bus route from Rotherham in the last years.

While the Rotherham terminus was still in Bridgegate, one of the ex Notts and Derby trolley buses, now painted green, is just moving to the turning point.

No 21 (FWX 905) a post war Sunbeam, standing at the Frederick Street Terminus.

On its journey to Conisbrough Low, a trolley bus turns off Grafton Bridge near the Rotherham depot. *Courtesy D Packer*

Commissioners for licences to operate P.S.V's on the trolley vehicle routes. The Corporation immediately decided to apply for the same licences and in view of the complete change in the relations with the Company, to "brief counsel".

A Mexborough trolley bus No 10 (FWX 894) in an "all over" green livery, also near the Rotherham depot with the disused tram track still showing. *Courtesy D Packer*

No 31 (FWX 915) passes a quiet residential corner in Swinton. *Courtesy E A G Gadsby*

On the way to Rotherham, a trolley bus passes down Rawmarsh Hill . *Courtesy D Packer*

No 32 (FWX 916) In a typical suburban area. *Courtesy E A G Gadsby*

No 20 (FWX 904) on its way to Rotherham stands by a bit of useful "old Rawmarsh".

No 37 (JWW 375) The first of the final three new trolley buses of 1950 passes the Old Toll Bar depot with its mesh of overhead wires. *Courtesy D Packer*

A Trolley bus from Conisbrough Low at the junction from Conanby (Conanby High) branch

Rotherham's application for licences was dated 25 November 1953. They applied for authority to operate public service vehicles on the following routes:-

❖ From the Rotherham boundary to Conisbrough

❖ From Adwick Road junction at Mexborough to Victoria Road junction

❖ From Stocks Lane/Dale Road, Rawmarsh around Green Lane and Kilnhurst Road

❖ From St Nicholas Road, Kilnhurst to the brickworks in Kilnhurst Road

❖ From the junction of St Nicholas Road and Claypit Lane, along Claypit Lane and Thrybergh Hall Road to Kilnhurst Road

❖ From the junction of High Street Rawmarsh and Stocks Lane to Monkwood and Mutley Avenue roundabout

They also included in the application Route No 7 at Maltby. To operate buses from the junction of Miglet Lane/Duke Avenue to Firth Crescent at its junction with Queens Avenue.

The Mexborough & Swinton Traction Co proposed to provide between Rotherham and Conisbrough Low (Brook Square) a twelve minute service using low bridge double deck buses which would give 265 seats per hour as compared with 192 with the existing trolley buses. Between Rotherham and Mexborough they were to provide a 6 minute interval peak hour service. From Rotherham to Rawmarsh (Green Lane) they were to give an 8 minute peak hour service using 44 seat single deck buses which would give the residents 330 seats per hour in replacement of the trolley vehicle provision of only 256 seats. Finally they proposed a new service using the low bridge double deck buses from Rotherham to Monkwood with a normal frequency of a bus every 40 minutes. Although this was not public knowledge, the Company had already come to arrangements with "sister companies" for the loan or acquisition of 19 low bridge double deck buses if a settlement was not reached. They proposed to protect Rotherham Corporation with a minimum fare of 2d to Little Bridge, Parkgate, while passengers were not to be picked up or set down on the section between Rotherham and Rotherham Bridge.

At the December meeting of the Rotherham Council Alderman Caine gave a long statement regarding the through service between Rotherham and Mexborough. They had terminated the agreement with the Company which had not been altered since 1928. Under the agreement Rotherham operated one bus to the Company's seven or eight. For every passenger in the Corporation area the Corporation now got 1/2d - it had been one penny until October 1952. The main point of disagreement was the boundary between Rotherham and Mexborough & Swinton Traction Co territory, which Rotherham only received to Rotherham Bridge for fares but paid for route maintenance to Stone Row (Little Bridge) although the Company took the revenue from Rotherham Bridge, a difference of 1/5th of a mile, a cost to Rotherham of some £2,200 per annum.

Alderman Caine apparently did not know why Stone Row was the boundary. When Greasbrough was incorporated into Rotherham in 1937, the Mexborough company's route was never referred to - but at this time Stone Row became the Rotherham boundary with no change of the fare stage. The Corporation pointed out that their short portion of the long route was 6d per mile more profitable than the Company's section - yet the Company proposed to pay the Corporation from the pool at 2d per mile to which the Corporation had replied on January 7th that this was not acceptable and that the agreement should be for the Stone Row boundary. On January 30th the Company suggested a meeting between three representatives of each side to consider differences. On March 21 the Corporation wrote that they were willing to go to arbitration for a decision. They felt that the Company was trying to put them in the wrong. "It is not our fault that the Company's fares are so high that they themselves have got frightened of them". We have terminated the agreement because the Company is being unreasonable. We would not agree to a measure which would mean the Corporation was subsidising the Company, which has increased fares four times since the war.

In February 1954 Alderman Caine reported that progress had been made. The Company had agreed that if fare reductions had to be made, it would be on their section, and were now in a mood to make a new agreement. To this Mr O'Donnell replied with an open letter in which he wrote that Alderman Caine's statement was a surprise to him - it was Rotherham who had asked for the Company's consent to withdraw their notice to determine the through running agreement. By March 31 the Company had decided that the Corporation's suggested terms were quite unacceptable. They decided to apply for road services licences for the whole of the trolley bus system and to arrange for its total substitution. It was hoped to provide a new turning circle at Stone Row by the Corporation boundary to cover the company obligations while trolley buses continued to be operated. The bus operation into Rotherham would be provided with a minimum protective 2d fare inside Rotherham, with no picking up or setting down between Stone Row and the Rotherham terminus. It was noted at this time that the Ministry had approved the turning circle at Roanwood Avenue at Swinton but refused permission for that at Hawley Street, Rawmarsh. In the new circumstances it was decided not to proceed with the turning circle immediately and not to order the buses to replace the trolley buses until some settlement could be reached. At this stage both parties decided to accept arbitration, particularly with reference to the boundary point and the fare stage.

In March the Ministry of Transport declined to nominate an arbitrator in view of the arbitration clauses in the 1928 agreement. Finally in May a new agreement was ironed out - the Corporation to take all the receipts from passengers in its area and to pay the Company 2.2d per mile for its operating costs in Corporation territory. It was reported to Rotherham Council on 20 September that the Mexborough & Swinton Traction Co had commenced the service from Monkwood estate into Rotherham, and that the Company would shortly replace the trolley vehicle Rawmarsh (Green Lane) services with buses. This took place on 27 September 1954. In the accounts for November appeared a new item. Paid Mexborough & Swinton Traction Co £464.10.9d - Receipts adjustment - rising to £1,126 in January 1955 and £2,156 in March.

A new period now commenced. In 1953 six 44 seat Leyland Tiger Cubs were ordered to be fitted with Weymann single deck bodies. Before these were delivered the order was increased to ten, the four additions being replacements for the four ex Devon General buses. The ten new Leyland single deck buses Nos 40 - 49 were delivered between March and August 1954, the first two entering service on Saturday March 6th running on the Parkgate - Rawmarsh - Kilnhurst route. The next six of them were to replace the Rotherham - Rawmarsh (Green Lane) trolley bus section. The public were informed that the change would provide them with a "more practical and spacious bus". It was not stressed that it would also give a quicker service "with less buses". The second hand ex-Devon General buses introduced in June 1952 were sold in 1954, as soon as the new fleet was in service.

Mr O'Donnell announced in March that he was leaving Mexborough to take up the post of general manager of the Ashton Corporation Transport Department. He was succeeded by Mr D R Vernon on 30 April 1954, having introduced his replacement to the local councils before he left. Rawmarsh Council congratulated Mr O'Donnell on his new appointment and thanked him for his work for the Road Safety Council.

With the arrival of the new buses the Parkgate and Kilnhurst route was extended to a new terminus at the Woodman Inn, while two of the Leyland Cubs were used on a new route opened on Monday 16 August 1954 from Low Stubbin, the Monkwood estate and Haugh village direct through Parkgate to Rotherham. This, apart from the terminus being at Haugh Village not Brampton, was the route that Burrows had unsuccessfully applied for in 1950. When introduced, the new service, which was joint with Rotherham Corporation, although Rotherham did not join in the actual operation, was to have been with a bus to Low Stubbin every three hours, but in July Rawmarsh Council had asked for a service every quarter of an hour to Haugh. Finally the Company provided a 20 minute interval service. The local miners were asking for a service from Sand Hill to New Stubbin, which the Company agreed to provide by withdrawing the 1.10 and 9.10 p.m. Woodman - Parkgate journeys, to which Rawmarsh Council would not agree. In the event the Company provided a service to New Stubbin in August, but it was at once complained that the timing was unsatisfactory - it was running too late for colliers to get to work and too early for them to return from work. Rawmarsh Council decided to ask Mr Vernon to a meeting with them to discuss the service. At the end of April, the Council had been happy to agree these changes and also with the proposal to replace the Green Lane and Kilnhurst Road trolley buses "in due course".

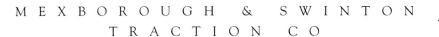

A series of illustrations showing No 50 (SWW 50) at various points on the Manvers to Ellershaw route. Also interior view and the "standee" seating arrangements.

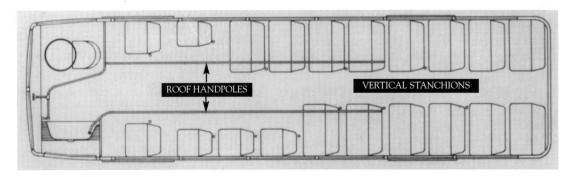

ROOF HANDPOLES

VERTICAL STANCHIONS

The Weymann front entrance bodies on the Leyland Cubs had the normal arrangement of seating for 44 passengers which, while ideal for normal off peak operation, left little room for standing at peak load periods. The low railway bridge near to Manvers Main was only just high enough to take single deck buses so that there was no possibility of converting to larger capacity low bridge double deck vehicles. The new manager decided that a bus with lower seating capacity but additional space for standing passengers might be the answer. The distance which "standees" would have to travel was small enough for there to be no question of them having to stand for more than twenty minutes or so, while it was better to be moving to and from work than waiting in the cold for the next bus - hoping that that also would not be full up. In 1955 two additional Leyland

Cubs were ordered to have larger engines than the existing ones and similar Weymann bodies but with seating for only 32 passengers and leaving space for up to 29 additional standing passengers. The design was produced in consultation with the Ministry of Transport engineers to the special requirements for standee buses. The seats faced forward with all but two seats on the off side double, and only four on the near side double, the remaining seats being single. For the benefit of the standing passengers upright stanchions were provided by the near side single seats with straps hanging from rails on both sides. Incidentally the buses were 8 ft wide - the earlier objection to the six inch increase was now forgotten. The buses, Nos. 50 & 51, entered service in January 1957 with a dispensation from the Ministry of Transport. After a short trial period Mayor Eastwood personally came over to see the buses in operation. He was pleased with them and in March issued permanent authority for their use. These two were joined by a third, No 52, ,in October 1957 which was modified to provide for 34 seated passengers and only 27 standees. These buses were provided with conductresses - there was no thought of one man operation. At this time, particularly for use on these buses, Setright ticket machines were brought into use. When discussing the advantages of the buses, Mr Vernon noted that the Road Fund licence for a 32 seat bus was only £57.12.0d - less than half that for a "modern large capacity double deck bus". In July 1954 the manager was authorised to dispose of the six "wartime" Sunbeam trolley buses which were now redundant and, by November, Doncaster Corporation had purchased them for £1,200. There the single deck bodies were removed and the reconstructed chassis fitted with double deck bodies. It is interesting that in due course these bodies were transferred to run on Leyland PD2 chassis. It might be noted that nothing was ever said about the Mexborough company's earlier suggestion that their trolley buses would be worn out and need replacement by 1959 and 1960. A year later in 1955 it was agreed to dispose of five of the 1947 batch of Sunbeam trolley buses, three to be sold "forthwith" and the remaining two as soon as the two new standee buses were delivered. Nos. 12, 13 and 15 came off operating fleet strength, two were scrapped but No 13 was retained for driver training duties. In July 1956 it was agreed to dispose of as scrap, No 19 after sever accident damage. In March 1956, Doncaster Corporation agreed to purchase two more trolley buses (Nos. 14 & 18) for £200 each. They were sold at this price, though their book value was £967 each.

Apart from the new buses a coach, No 100 - OWU 660 was added to the fleet in 1955. This was another Leyland Cub but provided with a Burlingham 41 seat body - specially purchased for private hire operation. During the period a further second hand bus, No 90, FKO 81, joined the fleet, a Leyland Tiger with an Eastern Coachworks body built in 1939 which came from the Maidstone and District Company in 1955. The Mexborough company until now had not entered the private party, excursion and tours field. Tickets for the Yorkshire Traction Co tours could be purchased at the Mexborough & Swinton depots but joining the Yorkshire Traction Co parties usually entailed one or two bus journeys to Barnsley with a late return at the end of the day. In April 1955, Smart of Greasbrough and Riley of Westgate, Rotherham, made a joint application to the Traffic Commissioners for a licence to operate a service from Rawmarsh to Yarmouth

One of Riley's 1950 advertisements, noting his summer services to Skegness and Cleethorpes.

A 1956 Mexborough and Swinton advert for its day trips.

No.49 (MWU 149 was painted green as an ordinary service bus, but during its life it was fitted with more comfortable high backed seats allowing it to be used for private parties. *Courtesy D.Dodd*

which was granted. At this stage the Mexborough management entered into discussions with Sheffield United Tours representatives with a suggestion that they should negotiate with Smart to purchase his excursions and tours licences, and then for them to operate the services jointly. In the event, Smart was unwilling to agree and the negotiations ceased. The Mexborough & Swinton coach No 100 received in April 1955 was the subject of some local publicity, a South Yorkshire Times reporter having a free trip on the coach in May. In July one of the 44 seat buses was touring the district to advertise the advantages of booking private hire trips with the Company. At the same time an application was made to the Traffic Commissioners to permit the Company to run a total of 15 excursions with Rawmarsh, Swinton and Wath upon Dearne picking up points. The three councils were pleased to support the application which was for full day tours with an average journey of 200 miles and half day tours travelling around 90 miles. Smart and Riley opposed the application on the ground that the Company was entering into competition with their field of operations. Having supported the application in April, Rawmarsh Council in October decided to oppose it. During the summer of 1955 they complained that the Company had used hired buses of all sorts and sizes, with different colours and doors in different places, with destinations which were not given clearly. To add insult to injury there was an advertisement on the rear of one of "their abominations" - "Why not hire our luxury coaches?". All of which were provided whilst the new 44 seat buses were being used for "private excursions". It was also noted that with the 44 seat buses passengers had already been left on the Monkwood Estate route and that the Company now intended to operate smaller buses on the route. Nevertheless, the application

was granted except that Rawmarsh was not allowed as a picking up point - the new services being the subject of advertisement in May 1956. Rather belatedly in June Rawmarsh Council decided not to formally oppose the application - just no longer support it! In view of a further application for a fare increase, the Council decided at the same meeting, to set up a special Committee to consider the application which the Company had made in May. It was noted that the trolley vehicle fares had been increased on 1 January 1956 without any prior consultation and said to have been the first trolley bus fare increase since September 1952. The Company was able to do this because a clause in the 1954 Transport Charges (Miscellaneous Provisions) Act had authorised trolley vehicle operators to increase fares without any reference to the licensing authorities. It seemed that Parliament in its wisdom, when passing the clause had forgotten that there was still one Company operated trolley bus system. The clause had been made, knowing that municipal operators had to present their case to its Council before agreeing to any fare change. After the Rawmarsh Council protest at the Company's action, they had asked the Rother Valley Member of Parliament to raise the matter in the House and Mr Ernest Davies MP accordingly asked that the clause should only apply to municipal operators. He was unsuccessful.

The Company's application in May 1956, after the January trolley vehicle fare increases had not had the desired effect, was sent to the Traffic Commissioners for an increase in both diesel and trolley bus fares. The Company claimed that under the recent revaluation of their property the rates had been increased from £1,356 to £8,000 per annum. Also that since 1952 wages had been increased by 36% and the cost of diesel fuel and electricity 57%. In view of this the application was unopposed and the new fares were introduced from July 30. Workmen's fares were withdrawn, the special 4d fare from Stocks Lane was also withdrawn and the existing "bus" fares were made general over the trolley vehicle section. Basically the fares increased by a half penny up to the 5d fares and by one penny above.

At the end of 1956 came the "Suez affair" and by January 1957 this caused a fuel crisis, Mr Vernon informed the various local authorities that no extra peak load buses could be provided on the diesel bus routes. He suggested that if schools could start at 9.15 instead of 9.00 it would assist operations. However for once the trolley vehicles came into their own. They were not "fuel "restricted" and services could not only be maintained but additions could be provided where this would help. In the middle of this Dearne Council announced that they would support Wath upon Dearne Council in their application for a direct bus service from Thurnscoe to Sheffield. As usual none of the established operators were interested - just as had been the case when the Dearne District Light Railways were in operation for the years in the 1920s when a through tram route from Thurnscoe to Sheffield would have been possible. A summer through route to Sheffield Millhouses Park in those days would almost certainly have been a "money spinner".

In post war years there had been considerable new housing development at the Mexborough end of the system, with estates near to Manvers Main and at Conisbrough. In January 1954 it was noted that these areas were asking for improved transport facilities. The Company decided that trolley bus route extensions into the Ellershaw estate from the Conanby route and into the Highland estate near the Manvers terminus would be justified. It was felt that a Provisional Order to build these extensions could be obtained by the time they were ready to make them. It was felt that if the demand became too vociferous they would provide a temporary bus service. However by August 1955 it was discovered that the two extensions would cost a prohibitive £13,000. It was agreed to increase the Manvers and Conanby trolley bus services at once and add ordinary bus services through the estates as soon as possible. However in spite of the fuel restrictions, the Mexborough Company introduced a new bus route on Monday January 21 1957. Once again the Windhill Estate gained a bus service, but this time with more hope of success. The route ran from either Manvers Main or the Highwoods Estate - through Mexborough turning up Adwick Road into the Windhill Estate passing along Morton Road to Hirst Gate which it followed back to the trolley bus route along which it continued as far as Lewes Road going along Ellershaw Lane and thence to Poplar Grove, serving Conisbrough's Ellershaw Estate. Basically alternate buses started either from Manvers Main or Highwoods Estate, though there were variants at colliery shift times. The first bus in the morning at 4.25 ran direct along the trolley bus route to Poplar Grove from Mexborough, as did the first from Manvers Main at 5.30 to Poplar Grove. The last bus at 11.00 p.m. ran from Ellershaw (Poplar Grove) via Windhill to the Rawmarsh depot.

Early in January 1957 there was a joint meeting of Rawmarsh, Swinton and Mexborough Council representatives which had been arranged to discuss the

acquisition, as provided by Parliament at ten year time intervals, of the Mexborough & Swinton Traction Co . It is strange that at this late date, with the Rawmarsh (Green Lane) trolley bus section already converted, that thoughts of "Municipalisation" should arise. Unfortunately, or in retrospect probably thankfully, all four Councils involved, Conisbrough, Mexborough, Swinton & Rawmarsh had to agree to the purchase. Through the summer of 1957, Rawmarsh Council tried to persuade the other three to agree - but was unsuccessful. In November both Swinton & Mexborough Councils decided to have nothing to do with the proposal while at Conisbrough they were only prepared to pay their part of taking financial and legal advice. It is not known if it was intended to take over the whole of the Mexborough undertaking - presumably the only portion for which the Councils had purchase powers was the trolley bus section - the remainder was operated under authority from the Traffic Commissioners - not by Parliamentary Act authorisation. The Company officials seem to have kept a low profile through the period - when they were approached on their thoughts on the proposal - after the decision to take no action was made - an official at Rawmarsh depot said "The manager is away on business this week and he is the only person able to make a statement on the matter". It would seem that no "statement" was ever made - it was obviously not necessary.

During this period the Mexborough & Swinton Traction Co had carried on as usual, probably they never considered that the "take over" was more than "wishful thinking" on Rawmarsh Council's part. In January, only a couple of weeks after the Manvers - Ellershaw bus route was started, Conisbrough Council decided to write to the Company complaining that the trolley bus service through Conisbrough had been reduced, particularly that the very useful 7.00 am trip no longer ran. They wished to know how many and at what times had the trolley buses been "knocked off". In the same week a Yorkshire Traction Co Ltd double deck bus from Kilnhurst to Doncaster "crashed" into the front of No 4 Trent Terrace at Conisbrough. It also knocked one of the trolley bus wiring poles over. Amazingly the Mexborough & Swinton repair staff had been taking a pole to another place - not stated - and this was fitted as a replacement immediately and the Mexborough workmen, so conveniently present, soon had normal service in operation. The bus would take considerably longer being repaired.

At the February meeting of the Conisbrough Council it was reported that satisfaction had been provided by the Mexborough Company which had pointed out that the 7.00 am trolley bus journey was covered adequately by the new 7.00 am bus from Ellershaw, while the Company had agreed to reinstate the 8.30 am trolley bus from Brook Square to Rotherham. However in the next Council meeting - after complaints from the local miners it was decided to ask the Mexborough manager to meet their General Purpose Committee to discuss certain timings in the half hourly Ellershaw to Manvers service. The 1.30 p.m. and the 9.30 p.m. got the miners to work too late and they wished them to be re timed to 1.20 and 9.20. To catch the previous buses at 1.00 and 9.00 got them to work too soon. The Mexborough manager, would not agree to the ten minute alteration, but could manage up to six minutes without needing major timetable alterations - where the matter ended. The Council was pleased to agree to a proposal by the Yorkshire Traction Co for a new service which would have duplicated the Mexborough & Swinton Company's route for much of its length. Starting from West Street, Mexborough it was to go to Conanby via Castle Hill, turning at Conanby and returning to Brook Square from whence it was to go by way of Crookhill Road to Edlington.

Wath upon Dearne was still wanting a through bus service direct to Sheffield - and having no success with any of the local operators, wrote to the Yorkshire Area Traffic Commissioners asking them to arrange for the service. The Traffic Commissioners had a meeting with the operators who said that such a service would be competitive and uneconomic and they would not provide one. The Commissioner then wrote to Wath upon Dearne Council detailing the result of his efforts and noting that he had no power to direct any of them to provide a service.

The Mexborough Company had done quite well with its first season of "excursions and tours" - having carried 1,675 passengers. In May 1957 they applied to the Traffic Commissioners for an additional picking up point and for an increase in the vehicle allowance. Smart and Riley again opposed and for once the application was refused. Accordingly the Company surrendered its excursions licences in September pending the results of its appeal against the decision. An enquiry was held on October 10 at Sheffield, but the Commissioners stood by their decision. The Company then accepted that it could pick up only at Kilnhurst and Woodman Inn and applied for a new set of excursions on the Commissioners terms.

Meanwhile the Mexborough Company continued its slow expansion into the hinterland along its main line. On Monday September 2 1957 the 1,000 residents of the Swinton, Bow Broom estate at last got a bus service which saved them the one mile walk from the estate to the trolley bus route at Station Street, Swinton. The existing route from Parkgate through Kilnhurst and Piccadilly to Woodman Inn was again extended from the main line along Rookery Road, Church Street, St John's Road, Storey Road and Queen Street to a terminus at the Cresswell Arms in Bow Broom.

Having impressed the chairman of the Traffic Commissioners, the local "commuters" were far from happy with the new "standee" buses. In November 1957 there were complaints at the Conisbrough Council meeting about a bus which the residents had named the "Canyon Flyer". They referred to the bus which provided for 29 standing passengers, and objected that the "standee" gangway was too wide and passengers on the bus were being thrown about whilst middle aged and elderly people would not use it. Presumably since there were two of these buses, they both rejoiced in the title. The Company agreed to fit straps for the assistance of the standing passengers in addition to the stanchions. There was a court case when a driver was fined for "dangerous" driving with one of them. He turned a sharp corner too quickly while a lady and two children was not yet seated and they were flung in a heap across the wide gangway.

There was an application in November for a further increase in fares on the buses, which the Commissioners agreed to. It was stated for the Company that the national strike of bus personnel in July had badly affected their receipts with a fall of half a million passengers in the past 5 months. They were now allowed to charge 2d from one stage and 3d for two or three stages. In spite of the strong objections from Swinton Council the Company noted that they intended to ask for the same increases on the trolley bus routes.

In December the West Riding district surveyor reported that the road at the Adwick Road turning circle was in need of heavy repairs and wrote to the Mexborough Company for a contribution towards the cost. The Company were not feeling co-operative and refused to be helpful. There had recently been a heavy increase in fuel tax which was costing the Company some 3d per bus mile extra. What had been 9d a gallon in 1950 had now risen to 2/6d per gallon. The ageing trolley bus equipment was still liable to cause difficulties. In January 1958 there was a fault in the YEB power supply at 6.00 p.m. on a

Saturday night which was repaired for general distribution by 7.30 but, for some reason - unstated - power was not available to the trolley bus installation until midnight on Sunday. Diesel buses served the Conisbrough sections from the Old Toll Bar depot to which, from the Mexborough direction, normal service was provided. On Saturday June 29 the trolley wires under the Manvers railway bridge broke. The crews of the stranded trolley buses were praised for the way that they directed traffic while the overhead line team made the repairs. On 10th February 1958 the Company reduced the off-peak service, between 9.00 a.m. and 4.00 p.m. from the long-standing 15 minute interval to a trolley bus every 20 minutes on the Rotherham - Conisbrough (Brook Square) route. This would still give a 10 minute service between Adwick Road junction and Rotherham - but the local councils were not happy about the development. They hoped that at least this service interval could be maintained - although it was admitted that Denaby railway crossing was the big difficulty. It was remarked that here the crossing gates were shut for more than half the time, and road traffic was being continuously impeded. There was a slight alteration of the route in the Ellershaw estate from April 1st 1958 when the buses ran along Old Road and Chestnut Green instead of by way of Lovers Lane and Ellershaw Lane. In the same month, Conisbrough Council was upset by a decision of the Traffic Commissioners to allow a short extension at Conanby along the Old Road as far as Lockerley Avenue junction - only 365 yards - but the council had objected to the proposal. At the same time the Commissioners refused to permit additional Saturday morning buses between Conanby and Doncaster which the council had wanted.

The Adwick Road Terminus with Mexborough trolley bus No 28 (FWX 912) ready for the journey to Rotherham.

The local councils were still asking for the additional bus services to meet their particular need. In January 1958, Brampton Council decided to ask their adjoining councils, Wath upon Dearne, Rawmarsh and Wombwell to support their request for through buses to Rotherham. They decided to approach the area Traffic Commissioners and their local Member of Parliament to urge their case. Once again the local operators were not interested whilst the Commissioner said he could not alter Burrow's service to run into Rotherham. In August it was reported that a private bus owner had sent a questionnaire to 160 Old Denaby residents asking them to indicate the terms and say when a service was needed. Next month the Old Denaby Parish Clerk reported that a bus service was to be introduced from Old Denaby to Doncaster on Saturdays and Tuesdays and at least twice a day to Mexborough. It was wishful thinking - the services were not provided.

For the summer period of 1958 there was a change in the operation of Riley & Grant. In March Riley applied to the Commissioners to operate the Express Carriage routes which Grant had provided. He surrendered his licences for the services from Greasbrough to Blackpool and Scarborough and from Rawmarsh to Yarmouth - the Commissioners agreeing to licence Riley instead of Grant. In November 1958 the Mexborough Company announced that they intended to apply to the Commissioner for a further fare increase - the recent wage increase award was costing £5,500 per annum, while passengers carried had declined in the past nine months by over a million. Once again the local councils held a meeting to decide whether to oppose the applications. Conisbrough, Mexborough and Rawmarsh were for action - Wath upon Dearne Council decided to do nothing whilst Swinton, having felt that any opposition was a waste of time was persuaded to join. The inquiry was held at Sheffield on Wednesday 21 January - the Councils being represented by their clerks. The Company representative pointed out that the 18 trolley vehicles purchased in 1947 and the 12 in 1948 would soon be twelve years old and due for replacement in 1959 and 1960. This does not seem to have been relevant - but was accepted as a fact - though trolley buses usually had a much longer life - as was to be proved later. The Commissioners granted the fare increase.

Further route extensions were proposed by the Mexborough Company on December 1958. Mexborough Council approved of a proposed route to the Highwoods Estate from Mexborough. Buses were to proceed along the route to Manvers Main as far as the Plant Hotel where they would pass around the perimeter of the estate back to the trolley bus route by Manvers bridge. In agreement with approaches from the local branch of the miners union, certain buses would continue to Manvers Main at "pit times". In February 1959 Swinton Council agreed to support the miners in a request for a direct service from Swinton to Manvers Main either by a new service or diversion of an existing one. In March a meeting was arranged between Company and miners representatives to discuss this requirement.

In January 1959 the manager was asked to report on a proposal to abandon the trolley vehicle system and at the same time to consider the prospect for continued trolley bus operation for 10 more years. He was also authorised to sell trolley bus Nos. 16, 21, 21 and 24 at the best possible price. It was agreed to purchase an additional Leyland/MCW standard bus, subject to the operation by one man of standee buses. The new bus, No 54, was received in February and entered service on the 30th operating between the Cresswell Arms at Swinton and Parkgate. The bus had been arranged for one man operation - and was put on this route for a trial period of six months, operating without a conductor under an agreement with the road staff. The three "standee" buses had not proved too successful and during this year they were converted to more normal seating, Nos. 50 and 51 to have 37 seats and No. 52 36 seats, with provision for only 25 standing passengers. If not originally arranged for one man operation, they were so fitted, at the latest by early 1960, when the initial trial period was over and one man operation had definitely come to stay. In July the proposals for abandoning the trolley vehicles were approved.

A Leyland Atlantean with an M.C.W. body was on trial by the Mexborough & Swinton in May 1959 before any of the Mexborough "trolley bus replacement" Leylands were received. This was the "shape of things to come" passing the Kings Head in Swinton under the trolley wires. *Courtesy E A Gadsby*

In the beginning of October 1959 the local press understood that the Mexborough company had addressed letters to the local councils suggesting that the company was considering changing the Rotherham to Conisbrough route from trolley to diesel bus operation. When asked, Mr Vernon would make no comment - but later in the month at the Conisbrough Council meeting the members were told that the Company had written suggesting that they would like to introduce single deck diesel buses of the type already in use between Conisbrough and Manvers. These had already some 1,800,000 miles of satisfactory service to their credit. The councils decided to hold a joint meeting to consider reaction to the proposal. Meanwhile in September it had already been decided by the Company to purchase nine Leyland Atlantean chassis to be provided with Weymann 75 seat low bridge bodies at an estimated cost of £54,000. One was to be delivered by January 1960 and the balance in 1961. At the same time the manager was authorised to dispose of trolley buses No 23 and of No 7 in November. In January 1960 it was decided to order an additional two Leyland Atlanteans. The Company deposited a bill in Parliament on December 1959 to "authorise the Company to discontinue the running of trolley vehicles along all, or any, of their trolley vehicle routes". Section 5 of the Bill included "for permission to repeal certain existing enactments relating to the Company and certain provisions of the Rawmarsh U.D.C. (Tramways) Act of 1900". In January Mexborough Council had already agreed to the changeover, as did Swinton where it was considered that the trolley buses were out of date and they preferred the new diesel buses. Conisbrough Council had not yet considered the Bill, only Rawmarsh came out in opposition. They decided to spend some £500 on submitting a formal petition to Parliament in view of their statutory right to buy out the Company. Their opposition had no effect - by March 17 the Bill had already been passed by the House of Lords committee and was finally approved without any alterations on June 2 1960.

Meanwhile the Company's slow expansion continued. In November 1959 they applied to the Traffic Commissioners for permission to supplement the Conisbrough - Kilnhurst route - then operated only by the Yorkshire Traction Company - with additional buses operated by them during normal working periods by Kilnhurst Colliery and from Monday to Friday in school terms. So far as the trolley bus route between Conanby and Manvers Main was concerned, they informed the councils concerned that the route was already partially converted and that after finally closing the trolley bus operation, the route would be operated by an increase in the number of 42 seat buses of the present type.

In December 1959 the Company made a further application for permission to operate a service from Swinton, Piccadilly estate or alternatively Bow Broom estate to Mexborough, Windmill Crescent. To give the Manvers miners their service, certain journeys were to operate direct from the Piccadilly estate to Manvers to cater for shift and office workers at the Colliery. This application noted that the colliers journeys between Swinton and Wath upon Dearne (Manvers Main) would be by way of Valley Road, Broadway, Rookery Road, Church Street and Golden Smithies Lane. The licence was granted in March 1960 and bus stopping signs were erected over this section, but the service was not provided. There was an old wooden bridge in Golden Smithies Lane across the now disused and filled in Dearne and Dove canal which they could not pass over. Because of further housing development at the Rawmarsh, Monkwood Estate from February 1st the service to Rotherham was increased to every 15 minutes at peak hours while at Monkwood the route was split at the end of Monkwood Road with extensions of alternate journeys to Stubbins Lane end and to Thorogate via Hague Avenue and Lister Avenue. Peak hour service would be 30 minutes from each terminus with normally a bus every 40 minutes. At the same time consideration was being given to an alteration to the Rawmarsh, Green Lane service to give a direct route from Sandhill Estate to Rotherham. The new service from Windhill to either Bow Broom or Piccadilly (named Brookside) started on Wednesday 24 February 1960.

With the passage through Parliament of the trolley bus abandonment Bill the Company suggested the service alterations they proposed to make. They wished to extend the existing route from the Brook Square terminus into the Windmill Estate to continue via Windmill Avenue as far as Old Mill Road. So far as the Conanby service was concerned they were to divide the route at Gordons Lane, one half continuing as at present along Old Road, the other half to go round by way of Leslie Avenue and Locksley Avenue to its junction with Old Road. Conisbrough Council suggested that they would prefer an extension of the existing route from the Welfare Avenue terminus, passing along Denaby Avenue to a terminus at Oldfield Avenue. At Mexborough they had decided to discontinue the use of the Adwick Road turning circle terminus and to continue the route along King's Road,

Public Notices

IN PARLIAMENT SESSION 1959-60.

Mexborough & Swinton Traction

NOTICE IS HEREBY GIVEN that the Mexborough and Swinton Traction Company Limited (hereinafter called "the Company") has applied to Parliament for leave to introduce in the present Session a Bill (hereinafter called "the Bill") for purposes of which the following is a concise summary:—

1. To authorise the Company to discontinue the running of trolley vehicles along all or any of their trolley vehicle routes or any part thereof upon satisfying the Traffic Commissioners that adequate services of public service vehicles will be provided in their place and to provide for the determination of the powers liabilities and duties of the Company with reference thereto.

2. To provide for the removal of certain apparatus provided in connection with the discontinued services of trolley vehicles and for the use, sale or disposal by the Company of the apparatus so removed; to make provision as to the reinstatement of any highway in or under which any such apparatus was laid or placed.

3. To make provision whereby in lieu of apparatus being removed by the Company, certain apparatus shall become the property of the local authority of the district in which it is situate and certain of the apparatus may be purchased by the said local authority or by statutory undertakers and may be retained in situ; to provide for the determination of any obligations of the Company in relation to any such apparatus.

4. To provide for the removal by the owner thereof of any equipment or notice attached to certain standards provided in connection with the discontinued services of trolley vehicles.

5. To repeal the existing enactments relating to the Company (so far as not previously repealed) and certain provisions of the Rawmarsh Urban District Council (Tramways) Act, 1900.

On and after the 4th day of December, 1959 a copy of the Bill may be inspected and copies thereof may be obtained at the price of two shillings each at the offices of the Company at Dale Road, Rawmarsh, near Rotherham, Yorkshire, and at the offices of the undermentioned Solicitors and Parliamentary Agents.

Dated this 2nd day of December, 1959.

SYDNEY MORSE & CO.,
Alder House,
1, Aldersgate Street,
London, E.C.1.
Solicitors for the Bill.
REES & FRERES,
8, Barton Street,
Westminster,
London, S.W.1.
(8364)　Parliamentary Agents.

The Bill introduced in 1959 to authorise the abandonment of the trolley bus system.

Pym Road, Albert Road and Victoria Road. Mexborough Council agreed with the proposal - "provided the Company would meet the cost of any alterations to kerbs and roadways at the street junctions which may be required. They now announced that it was hoped to complete the changeover during the spring of 1961. On July 30 1960 the Company announced the delivery of a Leyland Atlantean double deck bus, the first of eleven on order to replace the single deck trolley buses on the Rotherham to Conisbrough route. The bus which cost some £6,000 seated 72 passengers and was described by the Company manager as "the most modern and best passenger service bus in the district". The buses, to be the new numbers 1 - 11 (7001 - 7011 WU) had bodies built by Weymann, by now the Company's usual body builder. In February the Company had received four more single deck Weymann Bodied Leylands, numbered 55 to 58 (YWT 55 - 58). These were normal type contemporary single deckers seating 42 passengers with normal accommodation for standing passengers - the large capacity "standee" bus was already "history". These new buses were designed for one man operation. In July it was agreed to convert 3 "further" buses to one man operation. It was also decided to install fluorescent lighting in the new Atlanteans and to provide them with illuminated advert panels. Another trolley vehicle, No 15, had already been listed for disposal in March.

In October the Company finally announced their proposed date for closing the trolley bus system. The Manvers route would go early in the New Year while trolley buses would cease to run from Conisbrough (Brook Square) to Rotherham on Sunday March 26 1961. At the same time it was noted that due to recent wage increases a further fare increase would soon be required but this would be held until after the new services were in operation and the financial effects of the changes were known. In January 1961 it was agreed to purchase one further Leyland Atlantean at an estimated cost of £6,500 and also, second hand from the Yorkshire Traction Company, a Ford Thames with a Plaxton coach body, new in 1959, for £2,700 numbered 102 - XWX 376. It could have been considered third hand since it started life, not with Yorkshire Traction but with Camplejohn. In May, after the conversion it was decided that two more Atlanteans would be ordered.

The Yorkshire Traction Company, possibly because of the Mexborough & Swinton route changes, announced in November that they intended to close the Thurnscoe and Wath upon Dearne route and direct it at Bolton to run via Adwick Lane into Mexborough. The change took place on December 4th with Wath upon Dearne Council objecting very strongly to this final ending to the old Dearne District Light Railways route from Thurnscoe, via Wath upon Dearne to Barnsley. It is noteworthy that the Yorkshire Traction Co service was only hourly by this time. The section of the light railway between Bolton and Wath upon Dearne had never suffered from bus competition - there was not enough traffic for it to have been worthwhile. The new Yorkshire Traction Co route did not run on Sundays.

Both Doncaster Corporation and the Yorkshire Traction Company originally objected to the Mexborough & Swinton proposed alterations at Conanby, but when withdrawing their objection, Doncaster Corporation asked Conisbrough Council to support their proposed application to provide a half hourly service on Saturday from Conanby (Lockerley Avenue) to Doncaster. Finally the Mexborough Company announced that all agreements had been made and the Conanby and Manvers trolley bus routes would now be closed down on New Years Day 1961. Increased diesel bus services would be operated on the Manvers - Highwood estate - Mexborough - Conanby - Ellershaw estate route from Monday January 2nd. The existing service to Welfare Avenue was altered to run from the Lord Conyers Hotel via Leslie Avenue and Chambers Avenue as far as the end of Lockerley Avenue. At the same time Mr Vernon, the Mexborough manager refuted rumours that the Company was intending to introduce "general" one man operation. He said that they had not suggested "any such thing". The local councils made arrangements with the Company to purchase such of the old trolley bus wiring poles as they required for lighting purposes at a cost of £4 each. Mexborough bought 28 of them, noting they had made a good bargain as compared with the cost of buying and installing replacement concrete poles.

In November the Company applied to the Traffic Commissioners for authority to operate buses from Rotherham to either the Windmill or the Ellershaw Estate, noting that if and when granted the existing trolley bus service would be discontinued. There was now no opposition and the licence was granted in January 1961. The final commercial journey of the trolley buses followed on Sunday March 26. Trolley Bus No 29 was cut down to open "toast rack" condition and with the Rawmarsh Prize Band installed, it lead the final procession of local dignitaries "etc." They travelled from the Old Toll Bar at Denaby to Rotherham - where they proceeded to Sheffield for the formal luncheon ceremony and addresses starting with one by Mayor F S Eastwood the Area Traffic Commissioner. Among the principal guests were Mr H C Drayton, chairman of the British Electric Traction Company. Ironically this was the last electric traction route under the BET aegis - which had started life under a different parent company - after BET had decided not to take the infant under its wing. The old equipment was soon disposed of. 12 trolley buses, Numbers 27 - 33, 35 and 36 passed to Bradford Corporation while the Teeside Railless Traction Board took Nos. 25 and 26. At Bradford the single deck bodies were replaced by new double deck ones, the two at Teeside were not operated - but the spares would have been useful.

After a short period of operation by the new buses, the Company issued a special pass to a reporter at the South Yorkshire Times permitting him to travel freely over the system to find out what the new service was like and, particularly, the general passenger reaction to the innovation. He found that the public was quite happy with the new buses but were confused by the route numbers which had replaced the old trolley bus route letters. In fact throughout the trolley bus period, Rotherham Corporation trolley buses on the route had borne route numbers and the Company had only brought the new buses into line, but passengers were used to the old A's B's & C's and found it hard to relate to 3s 8s and 9s. In fact one protester described it as a "packy's puzzle", particularly with respect to the new timetable. The only intermediate route times were at Rawmarsh Road depot and Adwick Road junction and passengers were missing buses and having long waits for the next. It was noted that times varied as between Monday to Thursday, Friday, Saturday and Sunday and they were never sure what time the bus would be at their stop. Finally they could not understand why buses would stop for as long as 10 minutes at the Mexborough depot or Woodman – and felt that to have so much time they must have passed points earlier than could have been anticipated.

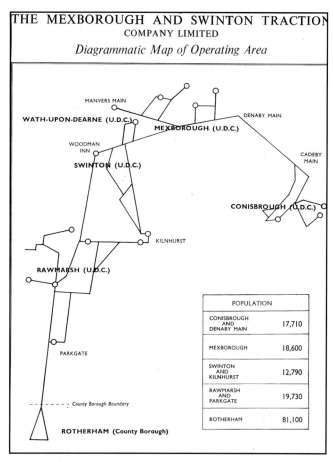

The Mexborough and Swinton routes after the trolley buses had gone.

Leyland Atlantean No 1 (7001 WU) taking passengers at the Woodman not long after the end of the trolley bus system.

In spite of these complaints the Company was short of double deck buses and in May 1961 decided to purchase a further two Leyland Atlanteans but these, Nos. 13 & 14, were not received until November 1962. Accordingly in November 1961 it was decided to purchase two second hand double deck buses from the Southdown Company for £180 for the pair. They took the numbers 15 & 16 (FCD 509 and 511) in the Mexborough fleet, and had rear entrance bodies – as compared with the front entrances of the Atlanteans. They had Leyland TD5 chassis and N & M E bodies. In the following July the manager was authorised to buy up four more at £120 each from Southdown as soon as they were needed.

Rotherham, Frederick Street terminus just after the conversion to Diesel bus operation. One of the Leyland/Weymann single deckers is ready to leave for Conisbrough with a Leyland Atlantean behind.

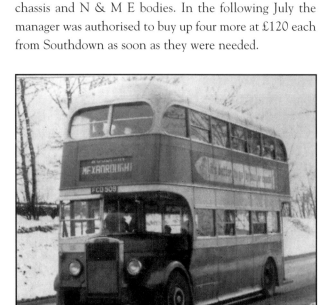

No 15 (FCD 509) joined the Mexborough fleet in 1961 *Courtesy M Fowler.*

Mexborough buses in Frederick Street, The double deck bus is on Route 7A.

No's 15 and 16 (FCD 509 and 511) were bought from Southdown in 1961. They only lasted a short time in Mexborough service being withdrawn in 1962. *Courtesy A B Cross*

The manager reacted to the timekeeping complaints by sending a letter to the district's Members of Parliament asking them to support a proposal for a flyover bridge at Denaby crossing. He pointed out that 300 M & S T Co and 150 YTC vehicles passed over the railway every day and that they had recently taken observations – the gates had been closed 64 times in 14 hours. The average time the gates were closed was 3.3 minutes – but it had been as long as ten minutes, The village of Old Denaby was finally provided with a bus service by the Mexborough Company on Friday May 25 1960, although the application for a route change was not published until 2 June when the Company asked for permission to divert buses on the Manvers Main to Ellershaw route to Old Denaby on Mondays, Fridays and Saturdays only twice a day at 2.30 and 5.22 p.m.. The Old Denaby residents then asked for the service to be made "daily". There was another "storm in a teacup" in September 1962. As a result of requests from the residents the terminal route at Mexborough of the Rotherham route was slightly extended to run round Pym Road, Kelvin street, Carlyles Street, Wellington Street back to the old Pym Road section. The alteration started at the beginning of September. Within a fortnight some residents decided to petition against the new arrangements claiming that the route was dangerous. However, after discussing the pros and cons at the next Mexborough Council meeting, it was decided that more residents were in favour of the change.

In November it was decided to buy three second-hand Leyland coaches from Southdown for £185 each. It was also agreed to dispose of the two ex-Southdown buses, Nos. 15 & 16 "at the best price obtainable". In due course, the two were scrapped by the Company. Four replacement double deck buses from Southdown arrived in the spring of 1963 and were numbered 15 to 18 (GUF 667,669,671 and 682). Number 17 was never operated and was scrapped at Mexborough; No 18 went to a dealers in November 1965, while 15 and 16 survived until 1966. The three coaches, Leyland PSU1/15 with Beadle 35 seat bodies arrived at the end of 1962 and were numbered 103 to 105. In November 1963 it was decided to purchase two 1952 Leyland Royal Tiger 41 seat coaches, again from Southdown, for £350 each. At the same time the manager reported that he could not justify the retention of the three Leyland/Beadle coaches and he was authorised to dispose of them "for a satisfactory offer". All three were scrapped by the company a year later. In July 1963 it was decided to purchase a Daimler Fleetline double deck bus with a Weymann body at the cost

estimate of some £6,900. Taking the number 19, it entered service over a year later in September, having cost £122 more than the original estimate.

No 16 (GUF 669) a Leyland PD2 with a Park Royal body was one of a batch of four purchased from Southdown in 1963. No 16 lasted in Mexborough service until 1966. *Courtesy P J Thompson*

The Dearne Valley Councils were still wanting the through bus service from Thurnscoe, through Wath upon Dearne, Woodman and Rawmarsh to Sheffield. In May 1963 Wath Council agreed to support a local independent proprietor, Phillipson and Sons trading as Dearneway Motors, when he made an application to the Traffic Commissioners for permission to operate a service from Thurnscoe to Sheffield. He asked for picking up points at Goldthorpe, Bolton, Wath upon Dearne, Swinton (Woodman), Rawmarsh and Parkgate. The application was immediately opposed by the existing operators, Sheffield and Rotherham Corporations, the Yorkshire Traction Co, the Mexborough & Swinton Traction Co and British Railways. The latter opponent was not a little ironic, since one of the reasons for Wath Council's support was because of British Rail's closure of Wath North station with its through rail route from there to Sheffield. The enquiry into the application was set for July 31, but prior to this Phillipson withdrew his application. He applied once again on 14 February 1964 – this time as a Stage Carriage operation, the earlier one had been as an Express Carriage route. He now asked for many additional picking up points, including Rotherham, Templeborough, Tinsley, Staniforth Road (Sheffield), with a Sheffield terminus in Castlegate. The new inquiry began on 13 April and was expected to last two days. After the third day, the Chairman of the Traffic Commissioners adjourned the hearing to a future date. For Phillipson it was stated that only two buses would be needed to give an hourly service – the journey from Thurnscoe to Sheffield, with all the picking up points, could be completed in under an hour. By the existing services, with all the changes, it took nearly two hours. For the opposition, the Yorkshire Traction Co had run a bus checking the time – calling at all the proposed stops took over 70 minutes – even a nonstop run took 51 minutes. Phillipson proposed a 5 shillings return and 2s 10d single. Finally the application was granted for an experimental twelve months period subject to the condition that, on journeys to Sheffield, passengers could be picked up only between Thurnscoe and Quarry Hill at Wath upon Dearne. The Commissioners expressed surprise that, though the service had been required for more than ten years, none of the local operators had offered to provide the service and had said that it was not needed and would be uneconomic. The service finally commenced on Monday October 5th with a service interval ranging between hourly and every two hours. Single deck, one man operated buses were provided. At the time the "Dearneway" fleet consisted of three double deck, a single deck bus and 16 coaches. When it became certain that Phillipson would be granted a licence, a meeting was arranged on 7 August 1964 when the managers of the Sheffield and Rotherham Corporation transport Departments and Mexborough & Swinton and Yorkshire Traction companies met to discuss the new competition in their area. The Traffic Commissioners had written to the four in June 1964 noting that the application had only been granted for a period of 12 months and had imposed an operational time of 65 minutes from Thurnscoe to Sheffield. At the meeting it was agreed that, with the conditions imposed by the Commissioners, the revenue from the route would not cover the operating expenses. However, since a further application by Phillipsons for more picking up points was expected it was decided to apply to the Commissioners for a new joint service from Mexborough to Sheffield to be operated on their behalf by the Mexborough company. Accordingly, having fought so hard in July to prove that the Thurnscoe to Sheffield service was not required, in October the Mexborough & Swinton Traction Co applied for a licence to operate a service from Mexborough to Sheffield. Phillipson objected and a hearing into the application was fixed for 13 January 1965. The reaction of the various local authorities to this move was one of ironic surprise. They were quite willing to support the application but could not avoid sarcastic comment as to the timing of the sudden decision that the service was required. The application was granted in February 1965, provisionally until 30 November 1966.

The service commenced on Monday 8 February, theoretically joint with Rotherham Corporation and Sheffield Joint Omnibus Committee. It was always operated by the Mexborough & Swinton with a bus every two hours from 7.32 until 21.32 from the Mexborough (Windhill Crescent) terminus. Unlike the restriction of picking up points imposed on Phillipson, there were a total of fifteen allowed to the Company. Having said that the Phillipson route could not run in an hour, the service from Mexborough could be performed – with all the stops – in 48 minutes.

There were a number of adjustments to the existing Mexborough Company routes in 1965. The Swinton Terminus of the route to Mexborough was moved from Brookside to Piccadilly, along Valley Road as far as Glebe Road. In May they asked for permission to alter the Rawmarsh circular route from Rawmarsh Hill to run on Blythe Avenue, Middle Avenue, Monkwood Road and Hague Avenue to Thorogate and then along Pipe House Lane and the Old Warren Vale Road and Kilnhurst Road to Claypit Lane and Green Lane joining the old route to Rotherham at Stocks Lane. A continuation of the Rotherham-Kilnhurst (Victoria Road) route along Victoria Street to Church Street to a new terminus at Queen Street Swinton was also applied for together with an alteration in Rawmarsh to the New Stubbin Colliery – Swinton (Cresswell Arms) route. Meanwhile the Mexborough Company had suffered with a series of strikes involving the new Mexborough - Sheffield service which was normally operated by one man single deck buses. Apart from Saturdays, traffic on this route was not great, indeed the Company claimed it was losing "about" £100 per week. The one-man operation was on a voluntary basis. However on Saturdays, traffic was so heavy that conductor operated double deck buses were provided – to which the men raised objections and accordingly went on Saturday strikes. These continued for 3 consecutive weeks during March, to the discomfort of the local populace, after which an agreement was reached. The service cannot have been so unprofitable since in January 1966 it was increased, except on Sundays, to run every hour. For accounting purposes, the route was divided into three portions by mileage; Mexborough to the Rotherham boundary 6.77 miles, Rotherham boundary to the Sheffield boundary at Templeborough 2.63 miles and in Sheffield 4.73 miles.

There was a further fare increase on 27 June 1965, which was followed by the usual acrimonious complaints from the local councils. The Company pointed out that this

Dearneway's advertisement in 1964 for the Thurnscoe-Sheffield service.

was the first increase since September 1961 and that the new wage agreement and the introduction of the 40 hour week was costing the Company £23,000 per annum. The fares increased by one penny between 3d and 6d and to "most" single fares over 6d. The Councils had a meeting to discuss the increases and decided in December to have a meeting with Mr Vernon and a director of the Company to ask for the re-introduction of the "overlapping" stages. They were wasting their time. From 1 January 1966 there were more of the route changes which had been suggested. In Rawmarsh the Monkwood Estate was linked up with the Green Lane route, with a ten minute service from Rotherham via Thrybergh Hall Road and Warren Vale Road at peak periods and a bus to Upper Haugh every hour. The extension of the Rotherham-Kilnhurst route to the Cresswell Arms, Swinton was to be on Fridays and Saturdays only. In February, Vernon arranged a meeting with the Mexborough Highways Committee to discuss provision of a bus service to Arnold Crescent, and also for a "two-way" circular service to cater for that estate and the Clayfield Estate. With the motorway being built, the Mexborough Company applied in May 1966 for permission to operate an express service from Mexborough to Leeds. The hearing for considering the application was fixed for 22 September and the opposition was particularly strong. The following decided to protest:- Yorkshire Traction Co; T Burrows & Son; West Riding Auto Co; Sheffield Joint Omnibus Committee; Rotherham Corporation and British Railways. In view of this the hearing was adjourned while

THE MEXBOROUGH & SWINTON TRACTION CO. LTD.

ROTHERHAM CORPORATION TRANSPORT DEPT.
SHEFFIELD JOINT OMNIBUS COMMITTEE

MEXBOROUGH - SHEFFIELD
LIMITED STOP SERVICE
Commencing MONDAY, 8th FEB., 1965
MONDAY TO SATURDAY

MEXBOROUGH (Windhill Crescent)	0732	2132
All stops to:		
Adwick Road Bus Shelter	0735 and	2135
Adwick Road Junction	0737	2137
City Bank	0739 every	2139
Don Hotel	0742	2142
Swinton Post Office	0744 2 hours	2144
Gate Inn	0746	2146
Woodman Inn	0748 until	2148
Rawmarsh Depot	0750	2150
Rawmarsh Post Office	0752	2152
Hollybush Street	0754	2154
Rotherham Bridge Inn	0758	2158
Templeborough	0804	2204
Tinsley Bridge (Broughton Lane)	0807	2207
Staniforth Road	0812	2212
POND STREET Bus Station	0820	2220
POND STREET Bus Station	0840	2240
Staniforth Road (Broughton Lane)	0848 and	2248
Tinsley Bridge	0853	2253
Templeborough	0858 every	2256
Rotherham Bridge Inn	0902	2302
Hollybush Street	0906 2 hours	2306
Rawmarsh Post Office	0908	2308
Rawmarsh Depot	0910 until	2310
Woodman Inn	0912	2312
Gate Inn	0914	2314
Swinton Post Office	0916	2316
Don Hotel	0918	2318
City Bank	0921	2321
Adwick Road Junction	0923	2323
Adwick Road Bus Shelter	0925	2325
All stops to		
MEXBOROUGH (Windhill Crescent)	0928	2328

SUNDAYS AND BANK HOLIDAYS
First bus from Mexboro' 1332 and then ever two hours to 2132
First bus from Sheffield 1440 and then every two hours to 2240
NO SERVICE CHRISTMAS DAY

PRIVATE PARTIES GO CAREFREE
by Mexborough & Swinton Coaches

CAREFREE COACH TRAVEL
CAREFREE because we take all the worries out of your hands.
CAREFREE because the price is right.
CAREFREE because your driver is your party's personal chauffeur. He is there to make your outing a success.

A letter, 'phone call or visit to our Rawmarsh office will receive immediate attention. DALE ROAD, RAWMARSH. Tel. 2351.

The 1965 advertisement for the Mexborough to Sheffield joint service

the proposal was given further consideration. It was not until September 1967 that a fresh application was made, this time jointly by the Mexborough Company, Rotherham Corporation, Sheffield Joint Omnibus Committee, Yorkshire Traction Co, West Riding Auto Co and Yorkshire Woollen District. It was stipulated that if the application were granted the earlier application by the Mexborough Company would be withdrawn. It was not until 30 April 1968 that the application was heard along with further joint applications for express services

from Sheffield to Halifax, to Bradford and Leeds. The whole to be known as the White Rose Services. They were granted on 11 October 1969.

In September 1966 the Yorkshire Traction Co decided to apply for permission to operate a service from Thurnscoe via Wath upon Dearne to the Woodman, whilst Rotherham Corporation, Yorkshire Traction Co and Mexborough & Swinton were to apply for a joint Rotherham - Wath upon Dearne service.

In July Mr Vernon, on becoming manager of the Yorkshire Woollen District company, tendered his resignation as manager of the Mexborough & Swinton as from 30 September. He was succeeded by Mr A J Price who was assistant manager to the Trent company. Strangely, after the date of his resignation, there was a report for October 12 1966 of the Swinton Councillors and Mr Vernon taking a trial run with a double deck bus along a section of the proposed route from Rotherham to Wath upon Dearne, going by way of Brig Drive, which was only 18 feet wide. After three attempts, they stopped the bus and held an emergency meeting there and decided the bus route would have to go along Warren Vale Road. At the end of October the Yorkshire Traction Co purchased Burrows' Rawmarsh-Leeds service. Mexborough & Swinton was not involved in the transaction which placed the Barnsley Company further into the Mexborough Company's area.

Phillipson was still not satisfied with the restrictions on his Thurnscoe to Sheffield service and, in 1965, he applied to the Traffic Commissioners for a number of additional picking up and setting down points. This application, with all the usual opposition, was first heard in January 1966, continued for two days in May, but it was not until October that his application was granted, and then only with three more picking up points. Meanwhile in April 1966 Yorkshire Traction Co applied for a service from Thurnscoe to the Woodman Inn. Phillipson opposed this application but the Commissioners provided the licence in October, by which time the Yorkshire Traction Co, Mexborough & Swinton Traction Co, and Rotherham Corporation had made a joint application to provide a joint service from Rotherham to Wath upon Dearne. In spite of objections from Phillipson and Wath Council, the licence was granted in April 1967. At a meeting of the Rawmarsh Council it was noted that the new Rotherham to Wath upon Dearne service was to be fitted into the Rotherham – Conisbrough service and that the peak service of a bus every 7 minutes would be reduced to every 10 minutes.

MEXBOROUGH AND SWINTON TRACTION COMPANY LTD.

REVISED TIMETABLES

WITH EFFECT FROM MONDAY, 3rd APRIL, 1967

Service No. 3—3A

ROTHERHAM TO CONISBOROUGH
Old Mill Avenue or Poplar Grove

Monday to Thursday · Friday · Saturday · Sunday

Service No. 9—9A

ROTHERHAM TO MEXBOROUGH
Carlyle Street or Arnold Crescent

Monday to Thursday · Friday · Saturday · Sunday

ROTHERHAM (Bus Station) to WATH-UPON-DEARNE (Tennyson Rise)

1st APRIL, 1967

A. J. PRICE, Manager

Conditions of Carriage and Passenger Regulations. Issued subject to the Company's official regulations and conditions.

PLEASE CUT OUT AND RETAIN

The new April 1967 timetable, with Mr A J Price as manager.

LET
Mexborough & Swinton Traction Co. Ltd.
DO THE DRIVING

SPRING BANK HOLIDAY EXCURSION PROGRAMME

SATURDAY, 27th MAY — Evening
MATLOCK
An evening drive via the picturesque Derbyshire countryside to MATLOCK for short stay .... 5.30 p.m. — 5/6

SUNDAY, 28th MAY — Full Day
NORTH WALES CIRCULAR
A Full Day scenic tour covering th. North Wales coast from RHYL to CONWAY going out via BUXTON and CHESTER. .... 7.05 a.m. — 23/6

SUNDAY, 28th MAY — Evening
RIPON
A scenic run to RIPON through beautiful Yorkshire countryside.
5.30 p.m. — 7.6

MONDAY, 29th MAY — Full Day
KESWICK & 6 LAKES
A full day tour to the LAKE DISTRICT covering ULLSWATER, THIRLSMERE, GRASMERE, AMBLESIDE & WINDERMERE with a stay at KESWICK (for DERWENT-WATER). 7.20 a.m. — 29.6

MONDAY, 29th MAY — Half Day
GRASSINGTON
A beautiful afternoon run through the heart of the DALES with a stay at GRASSINGTON. .... 1.00 p.m. — 10/-

MONDAY, 29th MAY — Evening
SLEAFORD
A pleasant evening drive into Lincolnshire .... 5.30 p.m. — 7/6

TUESDAY, 30th MAY — Full Day
LONDON AIRPORT
A full day outing via M.1 to LONDON AIRPORT for approximately 5 hours stay. Something for the young and old .... 7.05 a.m. — 27/6

TUESDAY, 30th MAY — Half Day
HARROGATE & KNARESBOROUGH
An afternoon drive to Yorkshire popular inland resort calling for a short stay at the picturesque town of KNARESBOROUGH. .... 1.30 p.m. — 9/-

CONNECTING BUS SERVICES FROM ALL PARTS

BOOK AT:
Company's Offices: DALE ROAD, RAWMARSH. .... Tel. Rawmarsh 2351
OLD TOLL BAR, MEXBOROUGH ...... Tel. Mexborough 2216

or following agents:-
D. SHELTON, 3 Queen Street, Swinton.
    Tel. Mexborough 2167.
ALLIED TRAVEL AGENCY, Mexborough.
    Tel. Mexborough 3102.
MR. DAGENHART, Wath Road, Mexborough.
    Tel. Mexborough 2550.
MR. SHREVES, 13, Helena Street, Mexborough.
    Tel. Mexborough 2703.

F. MURTAGH, West Street, Wath.
    Tel. Wath 2340.
J. RIX, 30, Highthorn Road, Kilnhurst.
    Tel. Mexborough 2361.
J. HUNT, Quarry Hill Road, Wath.
    Tel. Wath 2812.
GIBSON'S, William Street, Denaby.
    Tel. Conisbrough 1267.

(4944)

The spring 1967 Mexborough excursion advert.

In May 1967 it was reported that a new service was being considered between Rotherham and Windhill, Mexborough which would incorporate the three existing routes, Windhill-Cresswell, Windhill- Brookside and Parkgate-Cresswell with an hourly frequency instead of every 1½ hours.

During this period there had been great change throughout the bus industry. In March 1968 it was announced that Transport Holding Co had acquired the whole BET group shareholding. In April the Mexborough & Swinton Traction Co made application to the Traffic Commissioners for 10 major route changes

1) From Manvers Main and/or the Drill Hall to Conisbrough (Poplar Grove)

2) Mexborough (City Bank) to Old Denaby

3) Cemetery Road, Newhill to Old Mill Road or Bowman, Conisbrough

4) Rotherham to Rawmarsh (Manor Farm)

5) Mexborough (City Bank) to Clifton Village

6) Rotherham to Mexborough (Eden Terrace)

7) Rotherham to Conisbrough (Poplar Grove)

8) Rotherham Circular via Thorogate to Rotherham

9) Rotherham to Conisbrough Bowman

10) New Stubbin Colliery to Conisbrough (Poplar Grove)

All these were granted in June 1968.

The period of Mr Price's managership was to prove to be very short. There seems to have been no thought with the Mexborough & Swinton Traction Co directorate when he was appointed of the change to come. In fact they purchased a house for his accommodation when he was appointed. In December 1966 the directors approved of a plan for the complete modernisation of Rawmarsh depot at an estimated cost of some £30,000 while in January 1967 they discussed the possibility of disposing of the old Toll Bar depot at Denaby. In July, once Mexborough Council were interested in purchasing the site, they agreed to proceed with the disposal. By December it was on the market at a valuation of £7,000.

In the years since 1963, when the Daimler Fleetline was ordered, there had been much delving in the second hand market. After the four ex-Southdown double deckers arrived, it was agreed in November 1963 to purchase, once again from Southdown, two 1952 Leyland Royal Tiger 41 seat coaches for £350 each. They were numbered 106 and 107 in the Mexborough fleet. It was decided to dispose of the three Leyland/Beadle coaches at once, since the manager considered that their retention could not be justified. In January 1964 it was decided to dispose of No 17 (GUF 671) which had come from Southdown in 1963 but had not been operated by Mexborough & Swinton Traction Co. In May 1964 it was agreed to purchase a Leyland Lepard coach for about £6,000 – in July it was noted that it would be provided with a 36 foot Duple body. After which in November there was a return to the second hand market with an agreement to purchase, once again from Southdown, two Leyland PD2 54 seat double deckers for £120 each. In the Mexborough fleet the double deckers were numbered 17 and 20 (SCD29 and 39) while the coaches (LUF 639-640) became numbers 104 and 105.

The new Leyland Coach, No 108 (EWW 108C) was received in April 1965. It had a 49 seater body built by Duple (Northern). In January it was, again, decided to dispose of the three Leyland/Beadle coaches which were still "in stock" if not in use. On 1st June it was agreed they should order a further 49 seat Leyland/Duple coach at a cost estimate of £5,750. It was received in January 1966 and was numbered 109 (KWW 109D). In September 1965 the purchase of four more ex Southdown 58 seat Leyland double deckers, at a cost of £150 each, was authorised. Numbered 21 to 24 they were joined in November by a second hand 26 seat coach, also from Southdown. It was a Leyland with a body by Harrington and cost £250. On the arrival of the four double deck buses it was decided to dispose of numbers 15, 16 and 18 which had been at Mexborough since December 1963. After which in March 1966 a further Leyland/Duple 49 seat coach was ordered – at a cost estimate which had risen to £6,200. AT the same time a "provisional" order was given for six Daimler Fleetline for delivery in 1967. For the record it is noted that during the summer of 1966, the Southdown company loaned two Commer Avengers with Burlingham 33 seat coach bodies to the Mexborough & Swinton Traction Co.

On the arrival of Mr Price as manager he was authorised to convert the ex-Southdown coach, bus No 107, into a breakdown wagon at a cost not to exceed £200. A replacement programme was agreed in March 1967 when it was decided to dispose of the ten 1954 Leyland Tiger

Cubs, Numbers 40 to 49, and three ex-Southdown buses. As replacements it was agreed to purchase four second hand coaches from the Trent at £700 each, subject to these being available at the end of 1967. Finally four more Daimler Fleetline were to be ordered for delivery in 1968 – the order for these was confirmed in July at a price of £30,500. It was also agreed to buy three Fleetline 45 seat "semi-coaches" at £20,000 to be delivered in 1969. In November the decision to purchase three, not four, Bedford Harrington 41 seat coaches from Trent was cancelled. Instead three similar coaches, also Bedford/Harrington, were to be purchased from the Northern General Co at a total of £4,500 for the three. These, which were numbered 112-114 in the Mexborough fleet, were new in 1963.

A Mexborough & Swinton Advert in April 1968 listing its Easter excursion proposals.

THE YORKSHIRE TRACTION COMPANY, LIMITED.

THE MEXBOROUGH AND SWINTON TRACTION COMPANY, LIMITED,

REVISION OF CERTAIN SERVICES COMMENCING

MONDAY, 17th FEBRUARY, 1969.

Services 18, 18A, Newhill–Conisbrough

This service will operate between Newhill and Mexborough, Clayfield Estate, and will no longer operate via Highwoods Estate. A regular 20 minute frequency will be maintained as follows:—
Departing Newhill at 00, 20 and 40 minutes past each hour for Mexborough.
Departing Mexborough, Clayfield Estate at 10, 30 and 50 minutes past each hour for Newhill.

Service 21, Mexborough–High Green

This service will operate via Highwoods Estate, Mexborough, in both directions.

Services operated by The Mexborough and Swinton Traction Company, Limited.

Service 1, Ellershaw Estate–Drill Hall and Manvers

Mondays to Fridays –
Journeys will depart Oak Grove at 10 and 50 minutes past each hour for Manvers and at 30 minutes past each hour for Drill Hall (the 0430 and 0530 journeys will be extended to Manvers).
Journeys will depart Manvers at 20 and 40 minutes past each hour and Drill Hall at 03, 23 and 43 minutes past each hour for Oak Grove (the 0503 and 0603 ex Drill Hall journeys will commence at Manvers).

Saturdays –
Journeys will depart Oak Grove at 10, 30 and 50 minutes past each hour for Drill Hall (journeys before 0630 will operate to Manvers).
Journeys will depart Drill Hall at 03, 23 and 43 minutes past each hour for Oak Grove (journeys before 0703 will commence from Manvers).

Sundays –
Journeys will depart Oak Grove for Drill Hall at 55 and 25 minutes past each hour until 1125, then at 1203, 1233 and at 03 and 33 minutes past each hour (the 0455, 0525 and 05. journeys will operate to Manvers).
Journeys will depart Drill Hall for Oak Grove at 28 and 58 minutes past each hour until 1128, then 1205, 1235, and at 05 and 35 minutes past each hour (the 0458, 0528, 055 and 0628 journeys will commence from Manvers).
Journeys from Oak Grove at 1030 and 1430 and from Drill Hall at 1203 and 1503 will operate via Old Denaby on Mondays to Saturdays.

Service 4, Rotherham–Manor Farm

This service will become Circular in operation as follows:
Rotherham–Manor Farm via Greasbrough at 15 minutes past each hour.
                        via Rawmarsh at 45 minutes past each hour.
Manor Farm–Rotherham via Greasbrough at 15 minutes past each hour.
                        via Rawmarsh at 0510 then 45 minutes past each hour.

Service 5, Rotherham–Conisbrough via Kilnhurst

Mondays to Saturdays –
This service will operate hourly departing Rotherham on the hour for Conisbrough, and departing Conisbrough at 40 minutes past the hour for Rotherham.
In addition, hourly journeys will operate between Old Mill Avenue and Oak Grove, departing Old Mill Avenue at 08 minutes past the hour and Oak Grove at 24 minutes past the hour.
There will be no journeys at 0908 and 1708 from Old Mill Avenue to Oak Grove or at 0924 and 1724 from Oak Grove to Old Mill Avenue — the journeys arriving at Conisbrough at 0906 and 1706 will operate direct to Clifton.

Sundays –
This service will operate hourly between Cresswell Arms, Swinton, and Parkgate only, departing Cresswell Arms at 15 minutes past each hour and Parkgate at 45 minutes past each hour.

Services 6, 7, Rawmarsh Circulars will operate as follows:

Mondays to Saturdays –	Sundays –
Every 15 minutes to 0915	Every 40 minutes to 1200
then Every 20 minutes to 1530	then Every 20 minutes to 2210
then Every 15 minutes to 1630	2250 to Rawmarsh
then Every 20 minutes to 2210	
2250 to Rawmarsh	

Service 8, Rotherham–Mexborough

All journeys will now terminate at Highwoods Hotel and not Eden Terrace, Mexborough. The timetable will be revised as follows:
Mondays to Fridays –
Depart Rotherham 05, 25, 45 minutes past each hour.
Depart Mexborough 02, 22, 42 minutes past each hour.
Saturdays –
Depart Rotherham at 20 and 50 minutes past the hour to 0920, 0945, then 05, 25, 45 minutes past the hour.
Depart Mexborough at 27 and 57 minutes past the hour to 0957, 1022, 1042, then 02, 22, 42 minutes past the hour.
Sundays –
Depart Rotherham at 20 and 50 minutes past the hour to 1120, 1205, 1235, then at 05 and 35 minutes past the hour.
Depart Mexborough at 20 and 50 minutes past the hour to 1150, 1215, 1245, then at 15 and 45 minutes past the hour.

Service 9, Rotherham–Conisbrough

The timetable will be revised as follows:
Mondays to Fridays –
Depart Rotherham 15, 35, 55 minutes past the hour.
Depart Conisbrough 00, 20, 40 minutes past the hour.
Saturdays –
Depart Rotherham 05 and 35 minutes past the hour to 0935, then 0955, then 1 35, 55 minutes past the hour.
Depart Conisbrough 00 and 30 minutes past the hour to 1000, then 1020, 104 then 00, 20, 40 minutes past the hour.
Sundays –
Depart Rotherham at 20 and 50 minutes past the hour.
Depart Conisbrough at 18 and 48 minutes past the hour.

Service 28, Rotherham–Brampton

This service will be extended from West Melton to Brampton, Bull's Hea departing Rotherham at 00 and 30 minutes past the hour, and Brampton at 0 and 30 minutes past the hour. On Sundays the service will be reduced to hourly frequency departing Rotherham on the hour, and Brampton at 30 minut past the hour. All journeys will be 'LIMITED STOP' between Woodman In Swinton, and Rotherham, stopping only at Rawmarsh, Bus Depot, and Hollybus

Subject to the approval of the Traffic Commissioners.

FULL DETAILS ARE AVAILABLE AT COMPANY OFFICES.

The last Mexborough and Swinton timetable dated 17 February 1969;
The Yorkshire Traction already heads the advertisement.

In March 1967 a new Leyland PSU3/3R fitted with a Duple (Northern) 48 seat coach body was delivered. It took the number 110 (NWW 110E) in the Mexborough fleet. Six Daimler Fleetlines were delivered in December 1967. They were bodied by a firm, new to the Mexborough & Swinton Traction Co , Northern Counties M E Co with seating for 44 on top and 33 in the saloon. They were numbered 15-18, 20-21 (RWY 515-518F and 520F; 521F). In January 1968 it was decided to purchase a Ford Transit "minibus" for £900 and two second hand single deck buses to replace two second hand Leyland PD2 purchased in 1964. This was cancelled in March and purchase of either a BMC or a Bedford minibus at a cost of £900 was authorised.

In March 1968 it was noted that the Transport Holding Company had acquired the whole BET group and the transaction was completed by the month end. At the meeting of the Mexborough & Swinton Traction Co directors on 28 May 1966, it was announced that from 1 May the Yorkshire Traction Co had been providing management, Secretary/Accountant service for the Mexborough & Swinton Traction Co. This was the last meeting that Mr Price, the last Mexborough manager attended. Along with the Mexborough secretary and accountant, their resignations were accepted as from 30 April 1968. Mr Price accepted the post of traffic manager with an associated company. From May 1st Mr Hunt, the Yorkshire Traction Co manager became manager of the Mexborough Company as well, with Mr Roberts, traffic manager and Mr Brown deputy manager at Mexborough. For the time being the Mexborough & Swinton Traction Co continued in nominal separate existence. The local press took notice of the changes in May 1968 when they reported that Mr Alan Price had been appointed traffic manager of the City of Oxford Motor Services. Also that Mr Maurice Brown, who had been employed by the Yorkshire Traction Co for 45 years, had been appointed deputy manager of the Mexborough Company and that the Yorkshire Traction Co was assuming management of the Mexborough & Swinton Traction Co with Mr Hunt as General Manager.

The new management agreed at once to sell the 40 seat Ford coach No 102 (XWX 376); 26 seat Leyland (No 103) and a Leyland double deck bus. After long negotiations an agreement as to the bonus payments to staff for operating one man buses was signed by which they received an additional ten shillings per week. They also received a 15% wage addition for operating "non urban" services but argument continued as to whether "urban" service operation was worth only 17½% or a 20% addition, while one man operation of double deck buses could provide a further 2½% based on productivity.

In November 1968 the purchase of three single deck buses, to cost £26,000 was authorised. In July 1969 the order was passed for Daimler Fleetlines with Willowbrook bodies, to be delivered in 1970. At the same time a Leyland PSU3R/45 chassis to have a Plaxton coach body was ordered, also for 1970. In March 1969 the sale of four double deck buses to the West Riding Auto Co for £26,024 was agreed. These buses were four of the 1967 Daimlers with NCME bodies, numbers 15 – 18.

After the Yorkshire Traction Co took over control of the Mexborough & Swinton Traction Co in May 1968, day to day operation of the Mexborough undertaking continued as if it was still separate. Applications for route and fare alterations continued to be made by the Mexborough & Swinton Traction Co and it was only occasionally at meetings with the local council representatives that the Yorkshire Traction Co management was present to represent the Mexborough & Swinton Traction Co. In February 1969 a new service between Newhill, Wath upon Dearne and the Clayfield Estate at Mexborough was introduced, for which the local press congratulated the Mexborough & Swinton Traction Co management. On the "main line", Conisbrough to Rotherham in March, revised running times were introduced. Only 4 minutes "layover" time was now allowed whereas previously this had been 10 minutes. The staff was very displeased with the change, claiming that it did not allow them to make up time after service delays – particularly at Denaby railway crossing. Rawmarsh Council complained that they now had longer waits for buses and that when buses did arrive they were full. They were considering asking Rotherham Corporation to provide the services in the Rawmarsh area and to confer with the Regional Commissioner as to these complaints. There was then a meeting between representatives of council and company and a satisfactory conclusion was reached.

On 1 October 1969 the Mexborough & Swinton Traction Co officially handed over all their services and the 44-bus fleet to the Yorkshire Traction Co. At a meeting of the Mexborough & Swinton Traction Co directorate in July it had been agreed that "subject to the approval of the National Bus Co, all assets and liabilities would be transferred to the Yorkshire Traction Co. From 1 October the Mexborough & Swinton Traction Co became a non-trading company. Among the assets to become the

Yorkshire Traction Co property in due course were three single deck buses on order for delivery in 1970, three Daimler Fleetline single deck buses with Willowbrook bodies and a Leyland PSU3A coach to have a Plaxton body, also for 1970. The Yorkshire Traction Co now applied to the Traffic Commissioners for authority to operate all the Mexborough & Swinton Traction Co routes. Subject to their approval, the Mexborough & Swinton Traction Co licences would be surrendered. The

Yorkshire Traction Co was granted the licences and on 5 December 1969 in Notices and Proceedings, it was noted that the Mexborough & Swinton Traction Co licences were now surrendered. So far as the Mexborough & Swinton Traction Co staff were concerned, there was no change in their conditions – for the public the colour of its buses changed from green to red, while the word "Mexborough" disappeared from the bus sides.

The route details of the Mexborough and Swinton Co which were given in the application dated 12 September 1969 for the Yorkshire Traction to take over the Mexborough licences.

Yorkshire Traction Co. Ltd., of Upper Sheffield Road, Barnsley.

*BY.3/632.—Between Rotherham Bus Station and Brampton, Bull's Head, on the following route:— Outward: Drummond Street, Frederick Street, St. Ann's Road, Rotherham Road, Broad Street, Rawmarsh Hill, High Street, Blyth Avenue, Dale Road, Warrenvale Road into Swinton, Rockingham Road, Woodland Crescent to the Woodman turn left into Rockingham Road, Warrenvale Road, Wathwood Road, Sandygate, Burnham Road, Doncaster Road and Wath High Street, Montgomery Road, Barnsley Road, West Melton High Street, Oak Lea Avenue, Christchurch Road, Edward Road to Grove Road. Inward: Ouward route reversed. The service to operate daily throughout the year except that on Public Holidays the service may be reduced or augmented in accordance with public requirements all in accordance with the schedules deposited. Subject to the grant of this application the licence held by Mexborough & Swinton Traction Co. Ltd. under ref. no. BM.224/44, expiring 30.6.71 will be surrendered.

BY.3/633.—Between Rawmarsh (New Stubbin Colliery) and Conisbrough (Oak Grove), on the following route:— Rawmarsh (Stubbin Colliery), Greasborough Lane, Haugh Road, Blyth Avenue, Dale Road, Kilnhurst Road, Bellows Road, Green Lane, Claypit Lane, Thrybergh Hall Road, Kilnhurst Road, Dale Road, Blyth Avenue, Haugh Road, Glasshouse Lane, Victoria Street, Kilnhurst Meadow View, Fitzwilliam Street, Wentworth Road, Piccadilly Road, Fitzwilliam Street, Milton Street, Church Street, Station Street, Bridge Street, Rawns Lane, Swinton Road, Mexborough along High Street, Market Street, Oxford Road, Station Road, Bank Street, Doncaster Road into Denaby & Conisbrough, Station Road, Dale Road, Church Street, Old Road, Chestnut Grove to terminus at Oak Grove in accordance with schedules deposited. The service to operate daily throughout the year except that on Public Holidays the service may be reduced or augmented in accordance with public requirements. Subject to the grant of this application the licence held by Mexborough & Swinton Traction Co. Ltd. under ref no. BM. 224/42, expiring 30.6.71, will be surrendered.

*BY.3/634.—Between Rotherham Bus Station and Conisbrough (Old Mill Avenue), on the following route:— Rotherham Bus Station, Drummond Street, Frederick Street, St. Ann's Road, Grafton Bridge, Rotherham Road, Broad Street, Aldwarke Road, Barbers Avenue, Green Lane, Clay Pit Lane, Thrybergh Hall Road, Kilnhurst Road, Glasshouse Lane, Victoria Street, Kilnhurst, Wentworth Road, High House, Piccadilly, Piccadilly Road, Valley Road, Broadway, Rookery Road, Church Street, Swinton, St. Johns Road, Thomas Street, Bower Road, Queen Street, Church Street, Station Street, Rawms Lane, Mexborough, Swinton Road into High Street, Bank Street, Adwick Road, Princess Road, Harlington Lane, Morton Road, Hurstgate, Windmill Crescent, Hurstgate, Doncaster Road into Denaby, Doncaster Road, Conisbrough Station Road, Dale Road, Castle Street, Church Street, Morley Place, Marsh Street, New Hill, Brook Square, Clifton Hill, Windmill Avenue, Old Mill Road, Worthing Crescent, Windmill Avenue, Clifton Hill, Brook Square, New Hill, Marsh Street, Park Road, Chestnut Grove, Oak Grove. Inward: Outward route reversed in accordance with schedules deposited. The service to operate daily throughout the year except that on Public Holidays the service may be reduced or augmented in accordance with public requirements. Subject to the grant of this application the licence held by Mexborough & Swinton Traction Co. Ltd. under ref. no. BM.224/41, expiring 30.6.71 will be surrendered.

*BY.3/635.—Between Rotherham Bus Station and Rawmarsh Circular, on the following route:— (Service 6)—Rotherham Bus Station, Drummond Street, Frederick Street, St. Ann's Road, Grafton Bridge, Rotherham Road, Broad Street, Rawmarsh Hill, High Street, Blyth Avenue, Middle Avenue, Monkwood Road, Hague Avenue, Lister Avenue, Howgate, Warrenvale Road, Kilnhurst Road, Thrybergh Hall Road, Claypit Lane, Green Lane, Bellows Road, Rawmarsh Hill, Broad Street, Rotherham Road, Grafton Bridge, St. Ann's Road, Frederick Street, Rotherham Bus Station. (Service 7)—As above to Rawmarsh Hill, then into Bellows Road, Green Lane, Claypit Lane, Thrybergh Hall Road, Kilnhurst Road, Warrenvale Road, Howgate, Lister Avenue, Hague Avenue, Monkwood Road, Middle Avenue, Blyth Avenue, High Street, Rawmarsh Hill, Broad Street, Rotherham Road, Grafton Bridge, St. Ann's Road, Frederick Street, Rotherham Bus Station in accordance with schedules deposited. The service to operate daily throughout the year, except that on Public Holidays the service may be reduced or augmented in accordance with public requirements. Subject to the grant of this application the licence held by Mexborough & Swinton Traction Co. Ltd. under ref. no. BM.224/40, expiring 30.6.71 will be surrendered.

*BY.3/636.—Between Rotherham Bus Station and Oak Grove (Conisbrough), on the following route:— Frederick Street, St. Ann's Road, Grafton Bridge, Rotherham Road, Broad Street, Rawmarsh Hill, High Street, Blyth Avenue, Dale Road, Warrenvale Road to Swinton, Rockingham Road, Church Street, Station Street, Bridge Street, Rawms Lane, Swinton Road to Mexborough High Street, Bank Street, Doncaster Road to Denaby, Doncaster Road to Conisbrough Station Road, Dale Road, Church Street, Old Road, Chestnut Grove to Poplar Grove. Inward: Outward route reversed. Alternative route in Conisbrough, Conisbrough West Street, Old Road, Chestnut Grove, Oak Grove. Inward: Outward route reversed in accordance with schedules deposited. The service to operate daily throughout the year except that on Public Holidays the service may be reduced or augmented in accordance with public requirements. Subject to the grant of this application the licence held by Mexborough & Swinton Traction Co. Ltd. under ref. no. BM.224/39, expiring 30.6.71 will be surrendered.

*BY.3/637.—Between Rotherham Bus Station and Highwoods Hotel, Mexborough, on the following route:— Frederick Street, St. Ann's Road, Grafton Bridge, Rotherham Street, Broad Street, Rawmarsh Hill, High Street, Blyth Avenue, Dale Road, Warrenvale Road, into Swinton, Rockingham Road, Church Street, Station Street, Bridge Street, Rawms Lane into Mexborough, Swinton Road, High Street, Bank Street, Adwick Road, Arnold Crescent, Eden Terrace to Highwoods Hotel. Route in Mexborough for re-routing certain journeys Monday to Saturday (Route (a)—Adwick Road, Arnold Road, Edon Crescent into Elm Road Terminus, Highwoods Hotel. Route (b)—Adwick Road, Victoria Road, Pym Road, Kelvin Street, Carlisle Street, Wellington Street, Pym Road, Victoria Road). The service to operate daily throughout the year except that on Public Holidays the service may be reduced or augmented in accordance with public requirements. Subject to the grant of this application the licence held by Mexborough & Swinton Traction Co. Ltd. under ref. no. BM.224/38, expiring 30.6.71 will be surrendered.

BY.3/638.—Between Mexborough (City Bank) and Clifton Village, on the following route:— Mexborough City Bank, High Street, Bank Street, Doncaster Road, Denaby, Conisbrough Low Road, Brooke Square, Clifton Hill, Clifton Common Lane, Clifton Back Lane. Inward: Outward route reversed in accordance with schedules deposited. The service to operate daily throughout the year except on Public Holidays the service may be reduced or augmented in accordance with public requirements. Subject to the application being granted the licence held by Mexborough & Swinton Traction Co. Ltd. under ref. no. BM.224/37, expiring 30.6.71 will be surrendered.

*BY.3/639.—Between Rotherham Bus Station via Greasborough, Manor Farm and Rotherham Bus Station. "A" Route—Rotherham Bus Station, Frederick Street, St. Anns Road, Grafton Bridge, Rotherham Road, Parkgate Broad Street, Rawmarsh Hill, Rawmarsh, High Street, Blythe Avenue, Middle Avenue, Monkwood Road, Wilson Avenue, Haugh Road, Harding Avenue, Haugh Road, Symmonds Avenue, Low Stubbin, Higher Stubbin, Greasborough, The Wynns, Cinder Bridge Road, Greasborough Main Street, Scrooby Street, Mangham Road, Parkgate, Westfield Road, Greasborough Road, Broad Street, Rotherham Road, Grafton Bridge, St. Anns Road, Frederick Street, Rotherham Bus Station. "B" Route— Rotherham Bus Station, Frederick Street, St. Anns Road, Grafton Bridge, Rotherham Road, Parkgate, Broad Strtet, Greasborough Road, Westfield Road, Mangham Road, Greasborough Scrooby Street, Main Street, Cinder Bridge Road, The Wynns, Rawmarsh Higher Stubbin, Low Stubbin, Haugh Road, Symmonds Avenue, Haugh Road, Harding Avenue, Haugh Road, Wilson Avenue, Monkwood Road, Middle Avenue, Blythe Avenue, High Street, Rawmarsh Hill, Parkgate, Broad Street, Rotherham Road, Grafton Bridge, St. Anns Road, Frederick Street, Rotherham Bus Station in accordance with schedules deposited. The service to operate daily throughout the year except on Public Holidays the service may be reduced or augmented in accordance with public requirements. Subject to the grant of this application the licence held by Mexborough & Swinton Traction Co. Ltd. under ref. no. BM.224/36, expiring 30.6.71 will be surrendered.

BY.3/641.—Between City Bank, Mexborough and Old Denaby, on the following route:— Outward: (City Bank), Mexborough, High Street, Bank Street, Doncaster Road, Denaby Lane into Old Denaby. Inward: Outward route reversed in accordance with schedules deposited. The service to operate daily throughout the year except that on Public Holidays the service may be reduced or augmented in accordance with public requirements. Subject to the grant of this application the licence held by Mexborough & Swinton Traction Co. Ltd. under ref. no. BM. 224/34, expiring 30.6.71 will be surrendered.

BY.3/642.—Between Manvers and Conisbrough (Oak Grove), on the following route:— Eden Terrace, Elm Road, Highwoods Road, Wath Road, Main Street, Mexborough, High Street, Bank Street, Doncaster Road into Denaby & Conisbrough, Station Road, Dale Road, Church Street, Old Road. Alternative route:— Conisbrough West Street, Leslie/Chambers Avenue, Lockesley Avenue, Chestnut Grove, Oak Grove. Inward: Outward route reversed. To operate daily throughout the year except on Public Holidays the service may be reduced or augmented in accordance with public requirements. Subject to the grant of this application the licence held by Mexborough & Swinton Traction Co. Ltd. under ref. no. BM.224/33, expiring 30.6.71 will be surrendered.

†BY.3/643.—Between Mexborough, Windhill Crescent and Sheffield, Pond Street, on the following route:— Windhill Crescent, Morton Road, Princess Road, Adwick Road, A6023 Woodman Inn, A633 Rotherham, A630 Attercliffe, Effingham Street, Furnival Road, Sheaf Street, Hamer Lane, Pond Street, Sheffield, in accordance with schedules deposited. The service to operate daily throughout the year except Christmas Day and Boxing Day. Subject to the grant of this application the licence held by Mexborough & Swinton Traction Co. Ltd. under ref. no. BM. 224/22, expiring 30.6.70 will be surrendered.

BY.3/640.—Between Newhill via Wath & Mexborough & Clayfield Court, on the following route:— Outward: Cemetery Road, Quarry Hill Road, Campsall Fields Road, Stump Crossroads, Fitzwilliam Street, Church Street, Roman Terrace, Wath Road, Mexborough Main Street, High Street Bank Street, Adwick Road, Princess Road, Harlington Lane, Morton Road, Hirstgate, Coniston Road, right into Clayfield View, Clayfield Avenue, James Street, Clayfield Court. Inward: Outward route reversed. The service to operate daily throughout the year, except that on Public Holidays the service may be reduced or augmented in accordance with public requirements. Subject to the grant of this application the licence held by Mexborough & Swinton Traction Co. Ltd. under ref. no. BM.224/35, expiring 30.6.71 will be surrendered.

*Operating jointly with Rotherham Corporation.

†Operating jointly with Rotherham Corporation and Sheffield J.O.C.

Rotherham Corporation Transport
The Last Years

Unlike Mr Fisher, his predecessor as manager, Mr K Griffiths was new to Rotherham and came to the town with his own ideas as to the undertaking's requirements and had to "settle in" before deciding on the future progress of the system. He was the first manager since Mr Sykes to have come from the engineering side of the passenger transport world, having started his working life as a technical assistant at Liverpool, progressing thence to be Chief Engineer at Bradford and Manager at Ashton under Lyne Transport Department.

He was 45 years old when he was appointed as manager of Rotherham on 16 July 1967, and all things being unchanged could have looked forward to a long period in charge of the undertaking. The "electric traction" era was over and half of the fleet was already made up of front entrance large capacity double deck buses. There was a period of some months before he took up his post on Wednesday 25 October, during which time Mr S Bloor, the traffic superintendent was in charge.

The Ministry of Transport had at long last decided to allow double deck buses to be "one man" operated. This entailed bus entrances being at the near front corner, adjacent to the driver/conductor who was provided with cash and ticket issuing equipment which would not interfere with the driving arrangements. Much more difficult were the negotiations with the road staff to reach agreement as to the operation and wages for the combined duty. As will be remembered, an earlier attempt to arrive at an agreement had been unsuccessful.

Mr Griffiths took over in the middle of trouble. The day after he arrived the road staff, having been refused an increase in wages, refused to work any overtime. Since 15/20% of all services were being carried by overtime working there was considerable inconvenience to the public, who suddenly had no way of telling if "their" bus would turn up or not. The trouble continued for the following week. The management informing the staff that to cover the deficiency, they intended to stop all Sunday services and reduce Saturday working to the minimum. The Transport Committee now decided to work the services on "emergency" schedules, with buses being switched between routes to cover gaps in services. After nine days the men agreed to work "flexible" services and agreed that they were now willing to negotiate a productivity agreement – at the same time warning that the "non co-operation" could easily move to a complete stoppage. Negotiation was difficult – with the men asking for a "local" agreement with the management refusing to move away from a new "national" agreement which was under consideration. Finally the men agreed to call off the overtime ban from Monday November 27, but with the proviso – only until December 16 if there was not by then satisfactory progress in the local negotiations for a productivity scheme.

Early in December 1967, Alderman Dyson, the chairman of the Sheffield Transport Department approached the chairmen of the Rotherham and Chesterfield Transport Departments with a suggestion that they should voluntarily merge the three into one undertaking. This suggestion was made in the light of the new Transport Bill which had just been published. Under its proposals it would be possible for the Ministry of Transport to impose a grouping of undertakings, which none of them might like. Rotherham councillors were appalled at the suggestion which would result in Rotherham passengers having to pay "Sheffield type" fares – which were generally higher. At the following Rotherham Council meeting in January it was now suggested that any merger with Sheffield Transport should be strongly resisted.

There had been a fare increase in Sept 1967 which was necessary because of the continuing increase in both operating costs generally and wage increases particularly. At the same time it was agreed to increase the fares on Saturday and Friday night buses after 11.15 p.m. from 9d to 1/- for adults. This was the first increase for the service since its introduction in August 1960.

Throughout 1967 work on the "Rotherham" section of the M1 motorway had continued, with much alteration being needed to enable Blackburn, and the works in that area, being provided with services. The Ministry of

Transport rewarded Rotherham with a grant of £3,700 to cover its costs. The new Tinsley Viaduct was opened on June 15th – by which time only the section of the M1 from Tankersly to Leeds needed to be completed – hopefully by autumn 1967. In preparation for this event, Rotherham had joined the consortium of local bus operators to take its share in the operation of express coach services. From Mexborough via Rotherham to Leeds, 38 miles was hoped to take 65 minutes – the service from Rotherham to Leeds, only 30 miles, was scheduled to be covered in 45 minutes at fares of 5/6d single and 10/- return. Mr Bloor commented that since they had no suitable coaches they would not provide vehicles for this operation.

Throughout the autumn of 1967 and spring 1968 was a period of strikes and "rumours" of strikes. Not until August was an agreement ironed out on a productivity bonus scheme. The bus crews were to have a bonus of 10/- a week back dated to December 1967 and a further 10/- back dated to June 13th. The 10/- bonus was to be absorbed into normal pay from January 1st 1969. On their pay packet for December 1968 the men were paid £47,000 in "back pay", on average of £30 per man. This pay-out was money that the Government had "frozen" during the intervening period. At the same time the

Corporation decided to withdraw a number of loss making Sunday services, whilst in July as an example, an application was made to the Traffic Commissioners to withdraw the Saturday 9.30 p.m. bus to Ulley on which only one person travelled by way of Whiston to Ulley - and the bus returned empty. On the operations side, the service to Leeds started on October 18 1968, whilst "Yorkshire Services" put on a direct route from Rotherham via Hendon to London on Sunday November 1st leaving Rotherham at 10.00 a.m. on Sundays and 9.10 a.m. for the rest of the week. Fares were from All Saints Square 29/- single and 46/- return.

With the continuing rise in costs the 1967 fare increases had not covered costs, with a loss for the year ending March 1968 of £41,000 and £46,000 in March 1969. Decimalization, "horrible word", was now being prepared for, and at Rotherham an entirely new fare structure was proposed. From July 6 1969 all fares ending in a half penny were removed – ready for the national withdrawal of that coin in August. Fares were related directly to mileage. 0.6 miles 3d; 1 mile 4d; and so on up to 1/7d for 10.4 miles. At the same time it was noted that the bonus schemes for both road and depot staff were now in operation, that further general reduction of off peak services were under consideration and that in the near

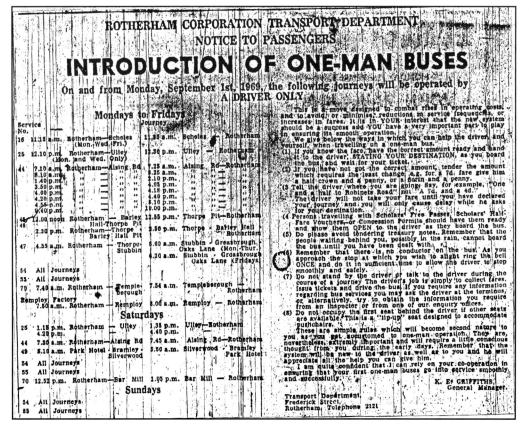

The notice dated September 1969 issued for the re-introduction, after nearly fifty years, of one man bus operation.

future all Sunday services would be one man operated. Negotiation with the men had been in progress all year – in March they had refused to give a two-month trial period to the system. They feared one manning could not operate to existing schedules and would need routes to be "time tested". Finally after route trials the men agreed to start, using single deck buses only, on September 1st. The first trial routes were those to Rockingham, Wingfield and some of the Alsing Road journeys. One man operation drivers were to have a 20% pay increase.

Under a new Government Transport Act, local councils could now pay a bus operator his costs for operating a loss making service. In the Rotherham Rural District, a small hamlet, Brookhouse, not far from Thurcroft it was then said that the hamlet "had never had a bus service". This was not quite correct, there was a reference, at this time, to a short lived trial service "about 1930" from Hooton Levitt through Brookhouse, presumably to Rotherham. This was provided by a gentleman named Bailey of Hooton Levitt; in 1929 there was a Wm. Bailey at the village, listed as a farmer in that year's directory. In January 1970, after negotiations between Rotherham Transport Department and the Rural District, it had been agreed to provide a service from Rotherham to Brookhouse on Mondays and Fridays with one bus in the morning and another in the afternoon. In February, the Rural District agreed to pay for any losses the Corporation may sustain in providing the service. In July the Rural Council decided to add to its subsidised bus services. It was agreed that a number of small villages between Maltby, Thurcroft and Ulley, which had never had any bus service should be provided with a service through Brookhouse, Slade Hooton and Hooton Levitt to Maltby and the Rural Council agreed to subsidise at up to £1,000 per annum. A local firm, Walsh's Coaches of Wickersley had agreed in principle to operate the service with a narrow Plaxton "Embassy" 20 seat bus with a journey each way daily and two journeys on Fridays and Saturdays. Walsh's, under the direction of the late Mrs James Walsh had in 1968 only recently entered the local coaching field. The council noted that the Brookhouse service was to cost £600 in the first year. It was decided to give further consideration to the Ulley - Maltby route "in the New Year". The Brookhouse service finally commenced on 7 September 1970.

In the first weeks of operation, only eleven passengers were carried; after six months only £12.08 had been taken in fares and it was noted that unless at least half the cost was covered by the fares, the government would not pay

back to the council what they had to pay the Corporation in subsidy. In August, the Rural Council gave Rotherham Transport the three months advance notice to terminate the services but withdrew them immediately with effect from 27 August 1971. At the same time it was decided that no action was to be taken with respect to the projected Ulley to Maltby route.

Walsh's of Wickersley intended to use FWT 74J, a Bedford with a Plaxton "Embassy" 20 seat body on the proposed service from Maltby through the Rotherham Rural District villages to Ulley. *Courtesy S Walsh*

Since Mr Griffiths' arrival there had been few changes in the services beyond minor extensions of routes to cover housing developments. In August 1967 the Maltby Manor Estate route was extended to Braithwell Road; in November the Fairfield Road route was discontinued, instead Chaucer Road was operated at its terminus section as a circular route – each way alternatively, while in December it was decided to extend the Wingfield Estate route a little further along the whole length of Nidderdale Road. In June 1968 it was decided to "modernise" the ticket collection system and as a start, probably with possible one man operation being on the cards, an initial order was placed for 25 "Almex" ticket machines, which were to cost nearly two thousand pounds. In December 1968, to cover development at East Herringthorpe, it was agreed to extend the route with a one way terminal circular portion to give a service to the "top end" of the estate – initially for a three month period. Additionally it was agreed that on the Dovedale Road route, all journeys would be by way of Herringthorpe Lane, Dovedale Road and Herringthorpe Road; this was an alteration of the "alternate direction" terminal arrangement then being used. Finally it was then agreed that the existing Leasegate Road terminus was dangerous and the route was extended to the Sitwell Arms at Whiston – alternate journeys being by way of Moorgate or the East Bawtry Road. After the April 1969 local elections the new Transport Committee decided that in future they would hold meetings "every other month" in June, August, October, December, February, and April. The Chairman, Deputy Chairman with the manager's assistance were allowed to authorise expenditure with the Committee, in effect, giving its agreement after the event.

No 212 (PET 212 J) a 1971 Daimler with a Roe front entrance centre exit body. The design was developed in the belief that it would help passenger flow and reduce standing time at stops. No 212 was snapped on its way to one of Rotherham's smaller industrial areas - Blackburn - with one of the factories, "Shardlows" just showing on the indicator. *Courtesy R.Brookes*

The first experimental one man operated routes had proved to be successful and after a little over two months the first routes, using double deck buses, converted to one man operation. These were route 15, East Herringthorpe; 26 to Aston; 17 & 18 to Blackburn and Shardlows and No 56 to Wingfield Estate via Fenton Road. This was followed on March 2 1970 with the addition of four routes in the Whiston area, two to Whiston via Moorgate and Leasegate Road, to Sitwell Park Gates and to Cowrakes Lane. One man operation had now definitely come to stay and had become the norm for bus operations. The Rotherham drivers had a wage increase of 20% for operating one-man single deck buses and 25% for operating one-man double deck buses.

There had been a few further route alterations. In June 1969 the circular end section of Dovedale Road was altered so that all journeys to Dovedale Road went by way of Herringthorpe Lane. In August, a sign of changes to come, Rotherham to Silverwood was discontinued and on Monday to Friday, Thrybergh journeys were diverted

to Silverwood – with no buses to Silverwood on Saturdays or Sundays. In October, the Leasegate Road service was discontinued and replaced by a route to Sitwell Arms at Whiston, travelling by way of Broom Valley. There was a minor terminal extension on 30 August 1970 when buses to Cowrakes Lane continued along Hall Close and Park Avenue to return to Cowrakes Lane - this would also assist with one-man operation. Similarly a year later, buses operating to Bramley only turned around Church Lane, Main Street and Cross Street to the Ball in at Bramley. In November 1971 the Kimberworth Park services were joined up with the Greasbrough, Rockingham and Wingfield routes to be operated by one man as circular services. One of the early conversions of the trolley bus routes had been the section between Wickersley and Maltby which, because of the Hellaby railway over-bridge, had prevented the use of double deck trolley buses. Only a few years later the railway was abandoned and in July 1971 the bridge was removed - it is noted that double deck buses had always been able to pass under on the way to and from Maltby. The new markets being built around Rotherham town centre, with one way traffic roads being introduced, caused some alteration to routes to and from the bus station. Buses had already left All Saints Square - it finally became available for pedestrians at the beginning of August 1971.

The change to decimal currency came on February 15th, but Rotherham Corporation held back the conversion until Sunday 21 February when the fare increases came into operation. The department said that this was so that people would have had their first decimal pay-day.

On 16 May 1971 the first section of the new bus station was brought into use, by which time over a third of the services were one man operated. From 31 October 1971, apart from the buses from the Maltby & Dinnington direction, all routes were using the bus station. It was given a formal opening ceremony on Friday 11 June 1971.

In 1970 the Maude proposals for changes to the municipal boundaries nationally, with suggestions for larger units, were objected to by both Sheffield and Rotherham. It was proposed that Sheffield, Rotherham and Barnsley be incorporated into a single authority. In August, in its place, Rotherham made its own proposals for local reform in the district by incorporating the Rural District Council and Rawmarsh into its boundaries. Finally, the new Local Government Bill was introduced in Parliament on November 4 1971. In March 1972 a Joint Steering Committee, with no powers, was formed for the proposed new South Yorkshire Metropolitan County Council. It was understood that it had 27 members. There were three each from Rotherham, Doncaster, and Barnsley with Sheffield having four members but it is not known who made up the difference in numbers. There was no reference at the time to what was to happen to the local passenger transport systems. By July the Rotherham representatives were reported as being angry with the Sheffield members, they felt that "Sheffield" was trying to be the dominant partner since they had suggested that the temporary headquarters should be in Sheffield.

On the home front during 1972 the future of the Herringthorpe Valley bus routes were discussed. It had been agreed that another "circular" route to cover this area could be provided by combining routes No 14, Dovedale Road and No 15, East Herringthorpe. Unfortunately only No 15 was one man operated and negotiators were taking their time in coming to an agreement over one man operation on No 14. When it was decided to convert the Treeton services to one man operation, the local parish council complained that the existing terminus was not suitable, since buses reversed at Bole Hill between two houses, and suggested a turning circle be built at the end of Bole Hill. Rotherham management thought that this solution was not tenable and felt that a new terminus should be provided to a curtailed terminus. It was not until July 1973 that it was stated that the East Herringthorpe circular route would be opened in September or October – there had been much difficulty in coming to an agreement over the alteration.

There was an unusual local transport development in July 1972 when Walsh's Coaches (Wickersley) Ltd applied to the Traffic Commissioners for permission to operate an Express stage Carriage service between Maltby and Holyhead by way of Doncaster Conisbrough, Rotherham bus station and Sheffield. The service was to run every Friday and Saturday from May until the last Saturday in September, with daily journeys from 21st to 30th December (Except Christmas Eve and Christmas Day). Buses were to return from Holyhead every Saturday and Sunday. The service was to have timing amended as required to fit in with the Holyhead to Dun-Laoghaire Mail Boat. There do not seem to have been any objections to the service, the application noted that it was not intended to pick up and set down passengers between Maltby and Sheffield. However, the service was never started. The "Irish trouble" was causing problems

and when a coach was blown up at this time on the motorway, Mrs Walsh withdrew the application. A service set up particularly for the local Irish traffic would seem to have been too vulnerable – so ended one of the few local attempts at this period for a small operator to enter the regular service field. It is noted that the firm was still a local coach operator until quite recently.

For the Maltby to Holyhead service, Mrs Walsh intended to use a Ford coach AYG 174H, with a Plaxton Paramount Elite 1 body. It is seen here to the left of Mr S Walsh, with his hand on the entrance door. *Courtesy Mr S Walsh*

The period of very high inflation had immediate effects on the department's ability to operate at a profit - wage awards were very much greater than normal and in November 1972 it was agreed that another fare increase was unavoidable. The wage increase that month amounted to some 20% on the basic wage and it was no longer possible to cover some of the cost by further service reductions. However, the Government now imposed a freeze on increases and the application to the Traffic Commissioners had to stand until after the year end. It was noted that the department would probably be "in the red" for the year end 1972/73. Finally in May 1973, the Council agreed that the application for the fare increases must be made at once. The minimum fare was now three pence but there was a general increase of at least a penny on all fares.

The elections for the new South Yorkshire Metropolitan County Council followed in April 1973 and its first meeting was at Barnsley at the month end. A Transport Committee was appointed, with Thwaites of Sheffield as its chairman and Ken Sampy of Doncaster as vice - chairman. At Rotherham it was decided in February that there should be some event to mark 70 years of Corporation transport, and finally the event was celebrated by a dinner, which seemed to be the acceptance that Rotherham Corporation Transport was coming to its close. Locally it began to be realised that the change was inevitable and in June 1973 there was a suggestion that, when the new South Yorkshire transport authority took over, the Rotherham buses might be painted cream. It got a cool reception when it seemed likely that Sheffield Corporation livery might be adopted. However, Mr Bloor said this was pure speculation as the South Yorkshire Passenger Transport Executive had not yet been set up, while the Rotherham chairman, Alderman G Brown who had decided to retire, thought that much more important decisions than bus colours would have to be made. In October it was suggested that Rotherham rate payers would have to foot the bill for part of the Sheffield Transport Department's losses - it was estimated that, for the year ended March 1975, this would amount to some £2.5 million. Rotherham transport, with its fare increase was still "paying its way" and would be handing over an undertaking which was debt free. The local paper commented "It seems that we are being taken for a ride - and a very expensive one at that." In December it was suggested that before the department vanished in April 1974, that the buses should be run free for a few weeks, but it was admitted that not much money would finally be handed over to the new South Yorkshire Authority.

In January 1974, it was agreed to start a new joint service with Sheffield Corporation between Kiveton Park and Rotherham. For this Kiveton Park R.D.C. agreed to make up any deficiency if the required agreed income was not reached. This new service commenced on Monday January 20 with three trips a day from Rotherham through Kiveton Park to Manor Way, Todwick with an hourly service on Saturday from 9.30 am to 5.30 p.m.. The cost to Rotherham of the transfer was still causing "pain" and in February it was suggested that Rotherham's £68,000 surplus should be retained by Rotherham. Already in January it was announced that Mr Griffiths was to become manager of the Sheffield District and Mr Bloor would take over as manager of Rotherham District. The functions were no longer the same - over these would be a number of directors giving the orders.

Rotherham Corporation Transport department ceased to exist from 1 April 1974 - it disappeared quietly at the end with hardly a valedictory word - but a quarter of a century later, the department's successful operation is still remembered with affection.

CHAPTER 5

THE FLEETS

Rotherham Corporation Tramways

1902/03 Nos 1-12 and 16-30. Built by the Electric Railway and Tramway Carriage Works - Open top double deck with extended canopies.

Nos 28-30 were fitted with top covers by Milnes Voss. December 1903. All but three of the remainder had "Leicester" type top covers built by the United Electric Car Company between 1906-13. At the start of the first World War, Nos 1-3 were still open topped. As the war progressed, they were fitted with top covers from trams lying derelict in the depot. In the years after the war most of these cars were re-built with six side window saloons. They were renumbered at times and the original numbers are not known. In 1920 seven new saloons were purchased, the cars being provided with top covers from scrapped saloons.

Nos 13-15, built by E.R. & T.C.W. - single deck. Rebuilt at E.R. & T.C.W. as top covered double deck cars in 1908. In 1920 a new saloon was purchased and fitted to one of these three, probably No 15 which lasted longer than the other two.

1905   No.31 - the water car and rail grinder. Built by E.R. & T.C.W. It was scrapped circa 1920.

1909   Nos 32-34 Built by United Electric Car Company. Large (4 window saloon) top covered double deck cars.

Nos 35-37 Built by United Electric Car Company. Smaller (3 window saloon) top covered "low bridge" cars.

1916   Nos 38-49 Second hand from Oldham Corporation. Single deck bogie cars. In 1918 No 44 was burnt out. In 1919 eight were sold to Walthamstow Corporation. One, as number 28, was fitted on to a Cravens single truck in 1921. Finally the remaining two were rebuilt with shortened vestibule bodies and fitted on to single trucks, either at this time or a little later being numbered 16 and 27.

One of the first batch of cars, No's-12 standing at the Pumping station terminus.

One of the first batch of "single ended" cars when new, passes a corner of Steel Peech & Tozer's Works - all now gone!

1916   Nos 50-59 second hand from London County Council, "B" class covered top deck vestibuled cars. New open canopy top covers were built by Rotherham for these cars in 1922. Re numbered 39-48 in 1922.

Nos 40-47 Sold to Sheffield 1926 - two scrapped at once remainder numbered 91-96.

1920   Nos 1-4 built by United Electric Car Company - Double deck open canopy top covered. It is not known in what sequence, if any, the Rotherham tram fleet was renumbered in the post "first war" years, particularly after the ex-L.C.C. trams were transferred to Sheffield in 1926. Certainly top covers were moved between cars. Before No 12, the last survivor of the pre 1914 cars, was scrapped in 1950, the numbers which the car had carried were noted. Starting from the last number which was still visible in the saloon the sequence was as follows:- 12; 10 and 15 whilst in the upper deck the numbers were 12,15 and 31. These were only numbers which had not been erased before fixing the later one. It is noted that the original car 31 was the water car whilst the original No 15 was one of the single deck cars with a larger body than the final No 12. Incidentally, a Rotherham car numbered 12 was weighed at Tinsley in February 1934 when the

new short ended cars were being delivered whilst "old type" Rotherham car No 15, the last of the large cars, was also weighed in October of that year.

At this time, Rotherham old type cars still in use on the Rotherham to Sheffield route included numbers 7; 9; 10; 11; 13; 14; 15 and 16. It is noted that the No 16 had been carried by one of the two Broom Road vestibuled cars and 13; 14 and 15 had all originally been single deck cars. As a child, the author first noted the two Broom Road single deck cars as 49 and 50 when he first took their numbers. When he took them later as 16 and 27, he made his own note that he had somehow made a mistake when he first saw these cars - not knowing of such things as car re-numbering. When he saw 49 and 50 he noted "flat roofed" cars as 1; 2; 3; 4; 10; 11; 13; 26 and 29.

1935   Nos 1-6. Built by English Electric Co. Double deck vestibule, single end cars.

1936   Nos 7-11 Built by English Electric Co. Double deck vestibule, single end cars.

1943   No 14. Second hand ex Leeds Corporation No 125A. Double deck extended canopy - top deck vestibuled by Rotherham.

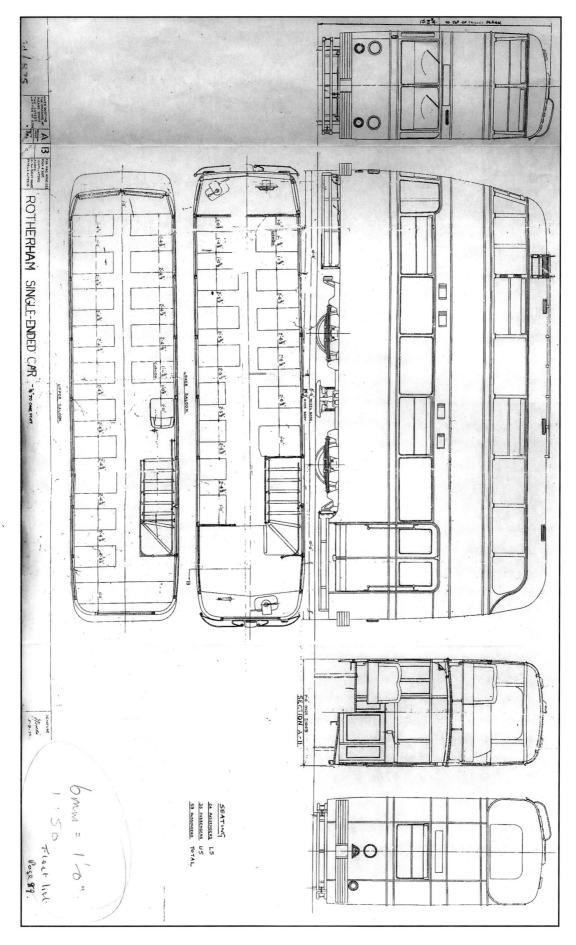

A copy from the English Electric blue print for the single end cars dated 5.9.1935.

Trolley Buses

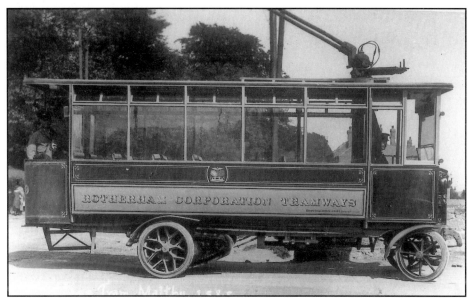

A trolley bus of the original fleet on the Maltby terminal circle.

1912   Nos 38-40 Single deck built by Milnes Voss, chassis by David Brown

1913   Nos 41-43 Single deck built by Milnes Voss, chassis by David Brown

Probably in 1916 renumbered T1 to T6.
In 1921 T1-T3 were registered ET 1922-24; T4 - ET 1925

1921   No T5 and T6 - ET 1926-27. Single deck bodies by Rotherham Corporation - Railless. Renumbered circa 1926 as 55 and 56.. Originally front entrance - re-built with centre entrance.

In c.1925/26 the author made the following notes:-
"Trackless trolley bus. Old type Numbers T6 and 56 ET 1927 - seats 32, seats are wooden backed. Four pneumatic wheels, made by R.E.T.. My diagram is of a front entrance body. Siemens controller BA4-0 UW 3-15 FA 2-0"

1922   T2 ET 2337 Straker Clough - Roe. Single deck front entrance rebuilt with centre entrance. Re numbered 52.

1924   Nos T3 and T4 - ET 2840-2841. Straker Clough - Roe. Single deck front entrance rebuilt with centre entrance. Renumbered 53 and 54. Later c.1933 - 18 and 41.

1925   Nos T7 and T8 - ET 3340 and 3341. Straker Clough - Roe. Single deck front entrance - rebuilt with centre entrance. Renumbered 57,58 (?) then 58 became 45 and then 42 (?) 57 to 17.

1927   Nos 50 - ET 3217 and 47 - 49 - ET 4818/20. Straker Clough - Roe. Single deck centre entrance. Sold in 1936 to Darlington Corporation.

1928   No 46 ET 4933. Guy 6 wheel - Roe single deck centre entrance. Renumbered 45 in 1939.

1929   No 43-45 ET 5284-6 Guy 6 wheel - Roe single deck centre entrance No 45 renumbered 44 in 1939.

In this year a Ransome's demonstration T.V. was in use for a short time and was numbered 42 while in Rotherham.

1930   No 51 ET 6020 Guy BT with a Guy single deck centre entrance body came to Rotherham as a demonstrator - and acquired. Renumbered 56 in 1938.

1931   Nos 39-40 ET 6607-6608; 19-24 ET 6609-6614; 25-30 ET 6615-6620; 31-38 ET 6621-66. Ransomes-Cravens single deck centre entrance. In 1933 Nos 39 and 40 were renumbered 55 and 56. From 1939 to 1948 there were a number of renumbers.

1933 Nos 52-54 and 57 - 58 ET 7880-7884. Guy- Cravens single deck centre entrance.

Nos 39-42 and 59 - ET 7885-7889. Guy with Roberts single deck centre entrance bodies.

1935 Nos 15-18 ET 9230-9233. Guy - Cravens single deck centre entrance. Renumbered 1947 to 27-30 and 1950 59-62.

1936 Nos 60-65 ET 9615-9620. Guy 6 wheel - Craven single deck 40 seat centre entrance. No 60 renumbered 66 in 1940. In 1947 Nos 61-66 renumbered 31-36. No 64 was rebuilt in 1945 by East Lancs Coachbuilders.

1937 Nos 14 - AET 901; 47-50 AET 902-905; 66 AET 906 and 203 AET 913 Guy 6 wheel - Cravens 39 seat single deck centre entrance.

Nos 67-70 AET 907-910; 201-202 AET 911,912; 204 AET 914 AEC 6 wheel - Cravens 39 seat single deck centre entrance.

1939 Nos 19-22 CET 80-83. Guy 6 Wheel - East Lancs Coachbuilders 38 seat single deck centre entrance. Renumbered 1947 to 55-58 and in 1950 56-58 to 69-71.

Nos 20-26 CET 84-87 A.E.C. 6 wheel - East Lancs Coachbuilders 39 seat single deck centre entrance. Renumbered 51-54 in 1947/8.

No 49 (ET 4820) a Stracken Clough with a Roe centre entrance body. This trolley bus received in 1927 was the last of a batch of four which were to be the prototype of the Rotherham fleet for many years. Petrol buses with bodies of this type also arrived in 1927.

No 46 (ET 4933). The first of the six wheel trolley buses which were purchased to operate Rotherham's share of the joint route to Mexborough. It entered service in June 1928.

No 17 (ET 9232) photographed in Cravens works prior to delivery. The 32 seat body was on a Guy BT 32 Chassis; it entered service in December 1935.

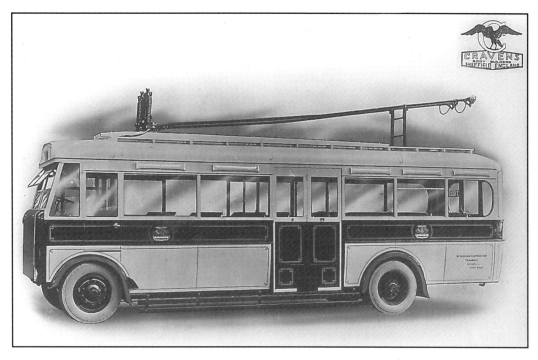

Body builder's illustrations of the first Cravens bodied Ransomes (No 31, ET 6607) delivered to Rotherham in March 1931. It travelled from Cravens works at Darnall, Sheffield early on a Sunday morning using Sheffield tram wires for power and trailing a skate in the tram rail to complete the electrical circuit.

No 70 - CET 480 was the first of the war time Sunbeams with East Lancs 39 seat bodies.

1940   Nos 70-77 CET 480-487. Sunbeam - East Lancs Coachbuilders 39 seat single deck centre entrance. Renumbered 1947 to 59-66 and in 1950 to 62-72

1942   Nos 82-89 CET 607-614. Sunbeam - East Lancs Coachbuilders 39 seat single deck centre entrance. Renumbered 1947 to 67-74 and in 1950 67 & 73 to 73 and 74.

1949   Nos 75-90 FET 335-350 Daimler - East Lancs Coachbuilders 38 seat single deck centre entrance. Nos 75,76,77,78,83,84 and 85 were fitted with Roe double deck bodies in 1956/57.

1950   Nos 91-94 FET 471-474, 1-24 FET 601-624 Daimler - East Lancs Coachbuilders 38 seat single deck centre entrance. Nos 7, 8, 11, 12, 14, 15, 16, 17, 18, 91, 91, 93 were fitted with Roe double deck bodies in 1956/57.

Photos of "the works" are rare. In operation, the bottom rear position was subject to weather damage.

Bus No. 70.
Date of Test 27/10/40.
Chassis No. 12229.
Total laden weight 11 tons 1 cwt. 2 qrs.
Schedule speed test over 14 miles route making all the usual stops (6 stops per mile); the route was completed in 58 minutes.
Acceleration test :
0.-30 m.p.h. in 11.6 seconds.
Climbing test :
Maximum speed ascending Whinney Hill (1 in 9) from a standing start, 22 m.p.h.
Hand Brake :
Tested descending Whinney Hill (1 in 9) hand brake brought vehicle to rest from 20 m.p.h. in approx. 100 ft.
Foot Brake :
Measured distance from 30 m.p.h., 53 ft. (on level road).
Retardation 18.5 ft. per second.
Efficiency 57 per cent.
Trolleybus operators will appreciate the significance of these figures, especially as the vehicle was fully laden for the purpose of the test.

The acceptance test details

THE NEW M.S.2c
SUNBEAM-BTH
TROLLEY BUS
CHASSIS

The Sunbeam chassis

CET 613 - a rear view.

No 88 (CET 613), a war time trolley bus delivered in February 1943. A Sunbeam model MS2C, it received an East Lancs 39 seat body. It was renumbered 74, as in this illustration, in 1947.

75 (FET 335) a Daimler with an East Lancs body. It was delivered in November 1949 - the first of the post war trolley buses after waiting a very long time!

No 75 - the interior looking forward from the centre exit.

No 75 - The interior looking to the rear.

No 39 (FET 342) started life in 1950 as a single deck trolley bus. It was fitted with a Roe double deck body in January 1957.

An offside view

A near side view - both taken at the Roe works before delivery.

No 21 (CET 82) a Guy BTX with an East Lancs body was renumbered, as here in 1947. It began service life just as the war started in 1939. The question is - was the vehicle behind the bus, apparently a trailer, a battery unit for manoeuvring away from the wires?

Motor Buses

The fleet numbers of all buses from 1913 to 1926 are not certain, many are taken by period and probability. Fleet numbers do not show in early photographs, and relatively few such photographs have been located. The author has yet to see a photograph of a bus up to 1922 on which a fleet number is visible. Similarly the "M" on buses to 1920 is not referred to in any known document and the author only had this letter allocation from Rotherham staff when he was a boy of some 12/13 years (c.1925/6). However he definitely noted a trolley bus still bearing the "T" at this time. The basic reason for belief in the change in fleet numbering to "T" and "M" in 1916 is that the second hand ex-Oldham tram cars were given tram fleet numbers in sequence from the existing highest Rotherham tram number 37 in 1916.

The early years of bus operations at Rotherham from 1913 to 1922 saw the change from the original open top double deck vehicles to experiments with one man operation, first with 14 seat then 20 seat small buses. With the arrival in 1923 of the first Bristols with Roe bodies, these two manufacturers gained most of the Rotherham contracts for the next decade. There were odd exceptions, two six wheeled Guys in 1927 with 39 seat Guy bodies, which only lasted for six years and were the only six-wheeled petrol or diesel engined buses ever used at Rotherham. The standard from 1927 was Bristol with 32 seat single deck centre entrance bodies, though in 1928, Rotherham Corporation built two bodies to the Roe design, whilst in 1930 Cravens provided three, so similar to Roe productions that they even included the distinctive Roe air vents above the saloon windows. From 1935 to 1938 Cravens gained the body contract, followed by East Lancs Coachbuilders from 1934 to 1948. For the first time since 1914 double deck rear entrance buses, Bristols with East Lancs Coachbuilders bodies, joined the single deck fleet in 1946. Two of the batch of four were provided with the new Bristol six cylinder diesel engines, in place of the Gardner five cylinder engines which had been the standard since 1935. The other two still had the five cylinder Gardner engines which proved somewhat "light" for double deck operations and they were soon given Bristol six cylinder engines in replacement. Further batches of Bristols with their engines were received in 1948 - also with East Lancs Coachbuilders bodies. These were followed by a period of change. Still using the Bristol chassis a small firm, Bruce, provided some 32 seat

centre entrance bodies using frames provided by East Lancs Coachbuilders in 1949 while another firm, Yorkshire Equipment Co, provided some double deck bodies, also using East Lancs frames. At this immediate post war period, there was a very great demand for new buses which could only be provided at quite long term delivery periods. At the same time under the terms of the 1947 Transport Act, the Bristol Co were not allowed to supply chassis to non "British Transport Commission" operators which meant that Bristols could no longer supply to Rotherham after existing contracts were completed. The last Bristols were supplied to Rotherham in March 1951. Rotherham therefore had to look round for manufacturers able to provide them with chassis. In the event, Crossley agreed to supply chassis which were provided with their double deck bodies in April and May 1949. In 1950, Bristol supplied the fleet intake in the shape of five KS6B, three L6B and five L5G, all were provided with East Lancs Coachbuilders bodies, double deck rear entrance Nos 100-104, single deck 32 seat centre entrance for the remainder, so that there were 3 single deck numbers 112-114 fitted with the six cylinder engines. It should be noted that the East Lancs Coachbuilders bodies were built at Bridlington by the subsidiary East Lancs (Bridlington) Ltd.

Two years later the chassis of Nos 112-114 were modified and fitted with East Lancs Coachbuilders double deck bodies. The practically new single deck bodies from these chassis were fitted on to reconditioned chassis of earlier buses. There was a considerable switching of bodies on to earlier chassis at this time whilst some bodies were completely reconstructed and fitted with 37 seat rear entrance bodies made up in the Corporation workshops. The annual report for the year end 31 March 1952 notes that "Three more single deck Bristol with six cylinder engines have been converted to double deck, in addition to the six which were started last year. The nine single deck bodies from these conversions have been reconditioned and fitted to earlier reconditioned chassis and engines. Nine more Bristol single deck are being reconditioned, and the first three are now having rear entrance 35 seat bodies built by East Lancs (Bridlington) Ltd. Next year it was reported that seven of the nine Bristol single deck being fitted with 35 seat bodies had been delivered, four by East Lancs (Bridlington) Ltd while the remainder had similar bodies built by S. H.

Bond Ltd of Wythenshawe, Manchester. In 1953/54, Bus No 143 after being badly damaged in an accident, had the chassis extended and was fitted with a new 37 seat rear entrance body built in the Rotherham workshops. No 143 had started life as No 153, BET 519 in September 1938. Next year, after an accident, bus No 159 had the same treatment - but the bus had started life in 1940 with an East Lancs Coachbuilders body, which had been replaced with a Bruce 1949 32 seat centre entrance body in 1951 before it received its final form.

Crossley provided further batches of double deck buses with their bodies in 1952 and 1953, the last of this type to be received. They were followed in 1954 with two batches of Daimler double deck rear entrance bodies by Weymann, a further newcomer to Rotherham. These were the first buses at Rotherham to be provided with fluid flywheels and pre-selector gear boxes. Five more with low bridge bodies were received in 1957. Charles Roe provided the low bridge bodies on three more Daimlers, while Weymann again were chosen for seven more standard bodies. Six new 45 seat single deck buses with front entrances on A.E.C. Reliance chassis were received - four with Weymann and two with Park Royal bodies. The suggestion that one man operation of large buses might be permitted resulted in the change to front entrance bodies and with the 1959 intake of three new A.E.C. with Weymann single deck bodies and twelve Daimler with Roe double deck bodies this became the standard, even though it was not until 1969 that one man operation was to start at Rotherham.

In 1955 Guy Motors had developed a new front entrance chassis named the Wulfrunian which initially had quite glowing press reports. It was designed for one man operation and Rotherham, on the look out for new developments, placed an order for three chassis in December 1959 to be confirmed by the end of May 1960. It was agreed to ask for tenders for the three bodies once the chassis order was confirmed. However it was decided in June that, owing to lack of other operators' experience with the chassis, the order was not confirmed. Instead, three A.E.C. Bridgemasters with 70 seat double deck Park Royal bodies were ordered. In October this order was increased by an additional two. They were received in 1961; two more A.E.C. Reliances with Roe 45 seat single deck bodies Nos 158 and 159 also came in this year. The new buses in 1962 and 1963 were all Daimlers, most with

Roe double deck front entrance bodies, though three of June 1963 tenders were accepted from A.E.C. for three Renown chassis, Daimler for four chassis and 7 double deck bodies from "Park Royal/Roe". In fact these are always described as being Roe bodied. These were received in 1964 at the same time as three more A.E.C. Reliances with another new body maker to Rotherham, the firm of Willowbrook who supplied the 45 seat front entrance single deck bodies. The order for these bodies was with "Duple Group Sales". From 1965 until 1972, with one exception, all the new buses were Daimlers, mostly double deck front entrance with Roe bodies. The exception was the arrival in 1966 of three A.E.C. Regal V with Neepsend double deck front entrance bodies. It was interesting that the order in June 1966 with Daimler was originally for nine chassis with forward engines and three Fleetline with rear engines. This order was amended to all twelve to be rear engined after it was noted that the new regulations allowed the top deck being sealed off and the lower saloon used as a single deck bus for one man operation. The last of the 1969 new buses were Daimler/Roe with front entrance and centre exit double deck bodies.

During 1968/69 ten of the remaining single deck buses were modified to be available for one man operations which finally started in Rotherham in 1969. Only two Daimlers joined the fleet in 1970 and these had Willowbrook single deck bodies. In 1971 and 1972 more Daimler/Roe with double deck front entrance and centre exit bodies were received as were nine Seddon with Plaxton single deck front entrance bodies. In the final year of Rotherham Corporation bus operation, twelve more Daimlers were added to the fleet, again with Roe bodies, but these reverted to the earlier double deck design with front entrance only and seating 78 passengers.

1913   Nos 44-46 ET 606-608. Daimler - Brush - open top double deck. Renumbered in 1916 to M1-M3. Nos M1 and M2 fitted with Bartle single deck bodies in 1920. Renumbered c.1922 47 and 48. Disposed of in 1924. In 1919 M3 was converted into a Tower Wagon and re-registered ET 1283.

1914   No 47 ET 796. Daimler with Brush open top double deck body. Renumbered in 1916 to M4. Fitted with Bartle single deck body in 1920. Renumbered 49 c.1922.

ET 607 (NO 45) Daimler/Brush A 'first war' photograph with the conductress in full uniform

1915   Nos 48-50. ET 982-984. Daimler - single deck bodies - maker unknown. Renumbered 1916 to M5-M7. Possibly in 1922 M5 and M6 to 50 and 51 and again c.1925 to 57 and 58. It is suggested that M7 (ET 984) was disposed of by 1920, although between 1920 and 1922 all three (one each year) were fitted with windscreens and side dashes on the driver's side.

1919   M8 ET 1450. (Note, since M3 was already converted to a Tower wagon - this fleet number was available). A.E.C. with a Bartle single deck body.

1920   M9 ET 984 (replaced M7) A.E.C. with a Bartle single deck body.

ET 2242 - No.54-1922 'T' type Ford. Body by Globe Pattern Works. *Courtesy A Taylor*

No 93 (ET 4603) a Bristol B with a Roe body was received in May 1927. This design was to be the Rotherham standard for the next decade.

1922   No 54 ET 2242 Ford - single deck 14 seat body - possibly built by Globe Pattern Works of Rotherham (2.2.1922).

No 56 ET 2339 Guy - single deck 14 seat body - probably taken from the Ford -Globe Pattern Works, Rotherham (29.6.1922).

Nos 57-60 ET 2339-2342. Guy with Guy 14 seat single deck bodies.
No 55 ET 2457 - Guy with Guy 14 seat body.

1923   Nos 61-63 ET 2794-2796. Bristol - Roe 20 seat single deck bodies.

1924   Nos 64-72 ET 2797-2805. Guy with Guy 20 seat single deck bodies. Nine Guy buses were ordered in September 1923. Guy took back 6 small 20 seat Guys at an allowance of £418 each plus 3 Daimler @ £300 each.

1925   Nos 73-74 ET 3214-3215 and Nos 80-82 ET 3346-3348. Bristol - Roe 20 seat front entrance single deck bodies.

Nos 75-79 ET 3216 and ET 3342-3345. Bristol - with Roe 32-seat front and rear entrance single deck bodies.

An off rear corner view of No 108 -ET 6046, one of the three Bristols with a Cravens Body.

1926 — Nos 89-90 ET 3349-3550. Bristol with 30 seat Roe single deck bodies.

No 83 ET 3858. Bristol with Roe 32 seat single deck body.

Nos 84, 85 ET 3859-3860. Dennis with Roe 20 seat single deck front entrance bodies.
Three Guys came from Hinton Bros after Barnsley & District purchased their business. These three came to Rotherham as their share of the transaction; registered WT 1222; WT 6644 and DA 9616, they may have carried Rotherham fleet number 86-88 respectively. All three were withdrawn by 1930.

1927 — Nos 92, 93 ET 4602-4603 and Nos 96-98 ET 4742-4744. Bristol with 32 seat Roe centre entrance single deck bodies.

Nos 94, 95 ET 4690-4691. Guy 6 wheel with Guy 39 seat single deck centre entrance bodies. Three Guy buses came from Rowley's Maltby service when Rotherham Corporation purchased the business - WT 6436; WT 7324 and WU 1427. The first two seated 26 passengers, the third possibly 31. However, the Corporation had an agreement that staff would not work as one man vehicles with seating more than 20 and therefore the two small capacity buses were disposed of at once. Theoretically they could have been numbered 92, 93, and 91 respectively.

No 109 (ET 6097) near side view of one of the three Bristols with Cravens bodies which entered service in April 1930.

No 115 (ET 8834) A Bristol JO5G with a Cravens body which entered service in May 1935, when "streamlined" painting was the latest fashion. It lasted at Rotherham for many years.

No 110 - ET 6224 - An offside front view.

No 111 - ET 6225 - the other one of the pair - a near side front corner.

1928   Nos 69-75 ET 4913-4919; No 101 ET 5231; Nos 102-103 ET 5347-5348. Bristol with Roe 32 seat centre entrance single deck bodies.

Nos 99-100 ET 5043 and ET 5216. Bristol with Rotherham Corporation built 32 seat centre entrance single deck bodies.

1929   Nos 64-68 ET 5467-5471; Nos 104-106 ET 5858-5860; No 86 ET 5956 Bristol with Roe 32 seat centre entrance single deck bodies. A Leyland, WT 8009 and two Guys - DT 196 and DT 444 came to Rotherham Corporation from

their share of the purchase of Guest's business. They were not operated by Rotherham.

1930   Nos 107-109 ET 6045-6047. Bristol with Cravens 32 seat centre entrance single deck bodies.

Nos 110-111 ET 6224-6225. Bristol with Roe 28 seat front entrance single deck bodies.

Nos 89-91 ET 6380-6392; No 61 ET 6383 and No 63 ET 6384. Bristol with Roe centre entrance single deck bodies.

1931 Nos 62, 76, 79, 80 and 83-85. ET 6600, 6601, 6602, 6603 and 6604-6606 respectively. Bristol with Roe centre entrance single deck bodies.

1932 Nos 77, 78, 81, 82, 87, 88 and 93. ET 7166-71. Bristol with Roe centre entrance single deck bodies.

1935 Nos 112-119 ET 8831-8838 Bristol with Cravens centre entrance single deck bodies.

Two buses were included in the purchase of T Green's service. It is very doubtful if they were used by Rotherham Corporation. A Dennis Lancet with a 32 seat rear entrance body given No 120 ANW 533 was received with the purchase of H Barker's business. No 121 WJ 95, a Leyland bodied Leyland came to Rotherham Corporation from Sheffield Corporation. Ex Kitson's services as its share of the Sheffield - Thorpe Hesley route.

1936 Nos 121-128 ET 9621-9628. Bristol with Cravens centre entrance single deck bodies. During the period 1943-1947 Nos 123-126 and 128 were completely rebuilt by East Lancs Coachbuilders.

1937 Nos 129-136 AET 629-636 Bristol with Cravens centre entrance single deck bodies.

1938 Nos 137-144 BET 347-354 and Nos 145-156, BET 511-522. Bristol with Cravens centre entrance single deck bodies. Nos 137, 140, 142 and 143 in 1951 received "second hand" Bruce bodies taken from 1949-1950 Bristols. These were also 32 seat centre entrance single deck bodies. No 153 after a collision, had its chassis extended and fitted with a Rotherham Corporation built 37 seat rear entrance single deck body in 1953.

1939 Nos 104-112 BET 901-909. Bristol with East Lancs Coachbuilders 32 seat centre entrance single deck bodies. Renumbered in 1949 - 147 to 155. As Renumbered Nos 147, 148, 150, 152, and 155 were provided with extended chassis frames and given new Bond 32 seat rear entrance bodies in 1953.

Nos 149, 151, 153 and 154 on extended frames were given East Lancs Coachbuilders (Bridlington) with 35 seat rear entrance single deck bodies in 1952.

1940 Nos 157-165 CET 440-448. Bristol with East Lancs Coachbuilders 32 seat centre entrance single deck bodies. Nos 159-162 were fitted with "second hand" Bruce 32 seat rear entrance single deck bodies in 1951. After an accident, No 159 had its chassis extended and was fitted with a Rotherham Corporation built 37 seat rear entrance body in 1955.

1941 Nos 100 and 101 CET 561-562. Bristol with East Lancs Coachbuilders 32 seat centre entrance single deck bodies. No 100 (as renumbered 165) was fitted with a "second hand" Bruce 32 seat rear entrance single deck body in 1951.

1942 Nos 102 and 103 CET 563-564. Bristol with East Lancs Coachbuilders 32 seat centre entrance single deck bodies.

1946 Nos 170 - 173. DET 370-373 Bristol K5G with East Lancs Coachbuilders 56 seat rear entrance double deck bodies. Nos 170 and 173 were given Bristol 6 cylinder engines 1951/52.
Note:- No.173 was renumbered 169

1948 Nos 173-178 EET 573-578. Bristol with East Lancs Coachbuilders 56 seat rear entrance double deck bodies.

1949 Nos 179-184 EET 579-584. Bristol l6B with Bruce 32 seat centre entrance S.D. bodies. In 1951 the chassis were modified to Bristol K6B standard and fitted with new East Lancs Coachbuilders double deck bodies. The single deck bodies were fitted on to pre-war reconditioned Bristol L5G chassis - already noted.

Nos 197-202 FET 351-356. Bristol K6B with Yorkshire Equipment double deck bodies. Nos 185-196 EET 885-896. Crossley with Crossley double deck bodies.
Note:- In the Bristol chassis type letters, B stands for Bristol and G for Gardner diesel engines.

1950 Nos 100-104 FET 800-804. Bristol KS6B with East Lancs Coachbuilders (Bridlington) double deck bodies. Nos 115-119 FET 815-819. Bristol L5G with East Lancs Coachbuilders (Bridlington) centre entrance single deck bodies. Nos 112-114 FET 812-814. Bristol L6B with East Lancs Coachbuilders (Bridlington) centre entrance single deck bodies. In 1952 the

BET 907, originally No 110, of the same batch as No.106 (BET 903) is seen at Sheffield (Pond St) before leaving for Doncaster. Now numbered 153 (in 1949) it is fitted with one of the East Lancs 35 seat rear entrance bodies dating from September 1952.

BET 907 An off side front view of the East Lancs (Bridlington) body.

chassis were modified to Bristol K6B standard and fitted with East Lancs Coachbuilders double deck bodies. The single deck bodies were fitted on to pre-war Bristol five cylinder engined chassis.

1951 Nos 105-111 FET 605-611. Bristol with East Lancs Coachbuilders (Bridlington) double deck bodies.

Nos 120-123 FET 820-823 Bristol with East Lancs Coachbuilders (Bridlington) single deck centre entrance bodies.

Nos 203-208 GET 503-508 Crossley with Crossley double deck bodies.

1953 Nos 209-214 HET 509-514. Crossley with Crossley double deck bodies.

No 148 (BET 902) as fitted with the Bond 35 seat rear entrance body.

No 171 (BET 371) was one of a batch of four Bristols numbered 170-173. They were delivered in December 1946, the first Rotherham double deck buses since the 1913 buses. Two of them 170 and 173 originally had Gardner 5 cylinder engines, the other pair used the Bristol 6 cylinder engine. East Lancs provided the bodies. *Courtesy R.Mack*

1954   Nos 215-229 KET 215-229. Daimler with Weymann double deck bodies.

1955   Nos 124-128 MET 124-128. Daimler with Weymann double deck bodies.

1956   Nos 129-131 HNU 819, 820 and 817 respectively were acquired second hand from Chesterfield Corporation. Leyland with Weymann double deck bodies dating from 1942.

1957   Nos 132-134 PET 132-134. Daimler with Roe low bridge double deck bodies.

Nos 230-236 PET 230-236. Daimler with Weymann double deck bodies.

Nos 160-163 RET 160-163. A.E.C. Reliance with Weymann single deck front entrance bodies.

Nos 164-165 RET 164-165 A.E.C. Reliance with Park Royal single deck front entrance bodies.

1959   Nos 166-168 TET 166-168. A.E.C. Reliance with Weymann single deck front entrance bodies.

Nos 135-136 TET 135-136. Daimler with Roe double deck front entrance bodies.

1961   Nos 137-139 and 140-141 VET 137-139 and YET 940-941. A.E.C. Bridgewater with Park Royal double deck front entrance bodies.

Nos 158-150 VET 158-159 A.E.C. Reliance with Roe single deck front entrance bodies.

1962   Nos 142-145 - 2142-2148 ET. Daimler with Roe double deck front entrance bodies.

No 189 (CET 441 a Bristol L5G with an East Lancs 32 seat centre exit body, entered service in June 1940. *Courtesy Roy Marshall*

NO 201 (FET355), a Bristol K6B with a body built by Yorkshire Equipment Co of Bridlington on East Lancs frames. A near rear illustration of No 201. It entered service in December 1949. *Courtesy Roy Marshall*

1963 Nos 146-148 - 2146-2148 ET Daimler with M.C.W. double deck front entrance bodies. Nos 149-153 and 95-99 - 3149 3153 ET and 3795-3799 ET. Daimler with Roe double deck front entrance bodies.

1964 Nos 88-90 - 5588-5590 ET A.E.C. Renown with Roe double deck front entrance bodies. Nos 91-94 - 5591-5594 ET Daimler with Roe double deck front entrance bodies. Nos 155-157 - 7155-7157 ET A.E.C. Reliance with Willowbrook single deck front entrance bodies.

1965 Nos 68-77 and 78-87 CET 68-77 C and DET 78-87 C. Daimler with Roe double deck front entrance bodies.

No.189 (EET 889) A Crossley with a Crossley body was new in May 1949. It is followed by No 173, (EET573) a Bristol K6B with a 1948 East Lancs body. *Courtesy RD Packer.*

No 162 (CET 445) of the same batch as No 158 received a body, secondhand in 1951 one of the Bruce 1949 bodies originally fitted to No's 179 - 184

1966   Nos 59-67 FET 50-67 D. Daimler with Roe double deck front entrance bodies.

Nos 129-131 FET 129-131 D. A.E.C. Regent with Neepsend double deck front entrance bodies.

1967   Nos 181-186 HET 181-186 F. Daimler with Roe double deck front entrance bodies.

1969   Nos 187-198 LET 187-198 G. Daimler with Roe double deck front entrance bodies.

Nos 199-208 NET 199-208 H. Daimler with Roe double deck front entrance and centre exit bodies.

No118 (FET118) A 1950 Bristol with an East Lancs body. *Courtesy of W Arnold*

No 113 (Fet 813) entered service in September 1950, a Bristol L6B with an East Lancs (Bridlington) 32 centre exit body
which was removed in 1951 and after alterations to the chasis it was provided with an East Lancs double deck body.
No 201 (FET335) moving out behind was Bristol K6B with a Yorkshire Equipment body on its way to Whiston

1970   Nos 169-170 NET 169-170 J. Daimler with Willowbrook single deck front entrance bodies.

1971   Nos 209-220 PET 209-220 J. Daimler with Roe double deck front entrance and centre exit bodies.

1972   Nos 221-235 VET 221-235 K. Daimler with Roe double deck front entrance and centre exit bodies.
Nos 171-179 WET 171-179 L. Seddon with Plaxton single deck front entrance bodies.

1973   Nos 101-112 OET 101-112 M. Daimler with Roe double deck front entrance bodies.

No 201 (FET 355), a Bristol K6B with a body built by Yorkshire Equipment Co of Bridlington on East Lancs frames. a. A near front corner view. *Courtesy Roy Marshall*

No 113 (FET 813) In February 1952 No 113 was fitted with a double deck body built by East Lancs. *Courtesy M Fenton*

No 's 112 (FET 812) and trolly bus 26 (FET 345) both started life with single deck bodies, the trolley bus received the body illustrated in 1956 after operating as a single deck vehicles from December 1949. No 112 however only lasted as a centre entrance single deck bus from September 1950 until February 1952 when it was provided with a East Lancs double deck body on an altered chassis. It's original body was fitted to an earlier 1939 chassis.

No 162 (RET 162) One of four A.E.C. Reliances Nos 160-163 with Weymann front entrance bodies. They entered service in October 1957. No 162 was standing in Barnsley bus station before travelling to Rotherham by route 27.

No 164 (RET 164) An A.E.C. Reliance posed outside Roe's office block in September 1951 before delivery to Rotherham. It is believed that the body was built by Park Royal and was fitted out by Roe's.

No 131 (FET 131 D) was an "odd" purchase for the Rotherham fleet; three A.E.C. Regents with Neepsend bodies which joined the fleet in December 1966. Neepsend Coachworks factory was in Sheffield; the firm was connected with East Lancs; they did not trade for very long. *Courtesy Roy Marshall*

The first Daimler Fleet-line to be added to the Rotherham Corporation fleet in October 1967.

No 182 (HET 182F) a Daimler CRG6LX with a Roe body standing in Sheffield Bus station before leaving for Maltby. The livery is the reverse of that on bus 185. Route No 87, which only passed through the southern outskirts of Rotherham, was the first to receive double deck buses in 1946.

No 113 (FET 813) In February 1952 No 113 was fitted with a double deck body built by East Lancs.
Courtesy M Fenton

No 169 (NET 169J) was one of a pair of Willowbrook bodied Daimler Fleetline which joined that fleet in December 1970. These were the first new single deckers to be received since 1964.

No 196 (LET 196G), a Daimler Fleetline with a Roe body, was new in January 1969. The most noticeable difference between this and No 185 of 1967 is in the new livery, white on the upper deck and blue throughout the front and saloon.

No 138 (VET 138). An A.E.C. Bridgemaster with a Park Royal body standing at the Rotherham, Frederick Street terminus before leaving for Mexborough not long after entering service in January 1961.

No 172 (WET 172L) A Seddon RU with a Plaxton "dual purpose " 44 seat body. This bus, one of a batch of nine entered service in November 1972, the last single desk buses to be received by Rotherham . The Seddon was a new product to be operated by Rotherham but the engine was the familiar Gardner , in this instance type 6HLX. *Courtesy Roy Marshall*

Mexborough & Swinton Traction Co
Tramways

Tram No 2 standing at Ryecroft, by Victoria Park, in the early Dolter Stud era.

Tram No 2 again at Parkgate. The two trams are on the "from Rotherham" loop with the driver at the wrong end. The indicator on the car behind is set for Parkgate.

1906   Nos 1 - 16. Brush open top double deck with Mountain and Gibson trucks. Twelve cars fitted with Brush low bridge top covers by December 31 1907.

Two further cars fitted with top covers December 1912.

Two cars - Nos 14 & 10 sold to Dewsbury and Ossett tramway July 1911 without top covers.

Two cars - Nos 7 & 15 sold to Dewsbury and Ossett tramway in 1929.

There was also a single deck works car - possibly built by Mountain and Gibson.

1908   Nos 17 - 20. Brush Top covered double deck with "Brush" 21E type trucks.

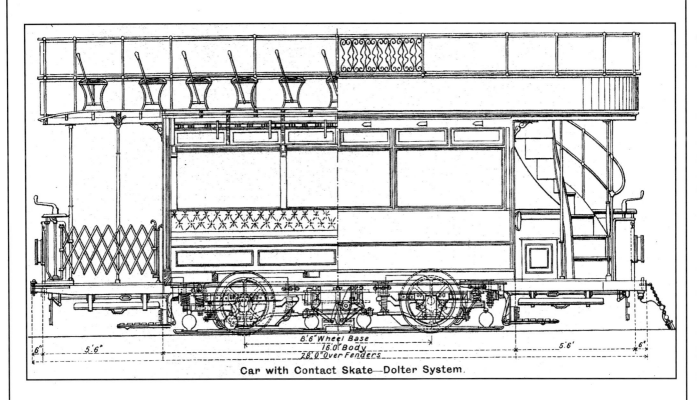

Car with Contact Skate—Dolter System.

A drawing of the proposed Mexborough tram with its Dolter equipment. The protuberance to the right bottom rear was a "brush" designed to blow the fuse of any stud left "live" after the tram had passed.

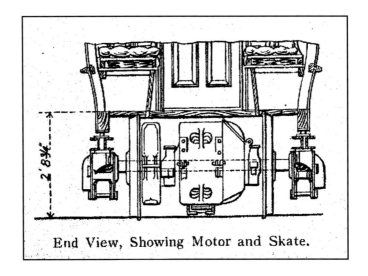

End View, Showing Motor and Skate.

Tram No 15 with the low bridge top cover. The side mounting for the trolley base shows up well.

Trolley buses

1915   Nos 21-23. Brush single deck. Chassis Daimler with Railless Electrical Traction Co modifications.

1917   No 24 Brush built 1913 - purchased by Mexborough & Swinton Traction Co from Stockport Corporation.

1922   Nos 25 & 26 WY 2743 and WY 3059. A.E.C. single deck with bodies by Strachan and Brown.

1924   No 32 - WT 7757. A.E.C. single deck - body make not known.

1928   No 34-39 and 40-48 WW 4688-4693 and WW 7872-7880. Garrett with Garrett single deck centre entrance bodies.

1929   Nos 49-60. WW 8790-8801. Garrett with Garrett single deck centre entrance bodies.

1930   Nos 61-63. WX 4440-4442. Garrett with Garrett single deck centre entrance bodies.

1937   Nos 64-69 RB 5568-5573. Second-hand ex. Notts & Derbyshire Traction Co. - English Electric with English Electric front entrance single deck bodies.

No 22 one of the original trolley buses. The location is not known, but it could be the Manvers terminus. The conductor looks too young to be "called up" while the two soldiers were probably on leave.

Stockport Corporation had three of these trolley buses, one of which came to Mexborough in 1917.

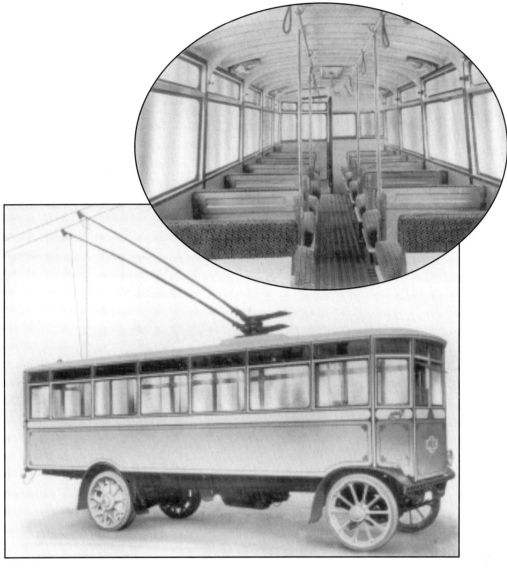

The demonstration A.E.C. trolley bus which the Mexborough Company purchased in 1922. It became No 25 (WY 2743)

1942   No 70 DY 5118; No 71 DY 5131; No 72 and 73 DY 5460-5461; 74 & 75 DY 5579 - 5580 - second hand from Hastings Tramway Co. Guy 6 wheel chassis with Ransomes single deck centre entrance bodies.

151   Nos 1-3 EWT 478-480 and 4-6 EWT 513-515. Sunbeam with Brush centre entrance single deck bodies.

1947   Nos 7-24 FWX 891-908 Sunbeam with Brush centre entrance single deck bodies.

1948   Nos 25-36 FWX 909-920. Sunbeam with Brush centre entrance single deck bodies.

1950   Nos 37-39 JWW 375-377. Sunbeam with Brush centre entrance single deck bodies.

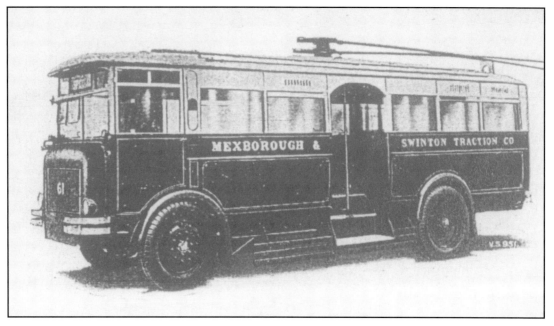

No 61 (WX 4440) which entered service at Mexborough in July 1930, was on show at the Hastings conference of the Tramway & Light Railways Association from June 11th to 13th. It is not known if it was demonstrated operationally under the Hastings wires.

Tram No 19 is just in the picture with trolley bus No 44 (WW 4693) leading "the last tram and the first trolley bus on the Rotherham to Conisbrough route".

Motor Buses

The 1910 Thornycroft charabane, probably standing at the Woodman terminus *Courtesy of A Taylor*

There are three tower wagons in this illustration, both the right hand and the left hand ones started life with the Mexborough Co as buses, Nos 28 (WY 4519) and 27 (WY 4589)respectively in 1922. They were converted to tower wagons in 1928. Ex No 27 was left with the front half of its body intact.

1910   May not have been numbered in the Mexborough fleet. A Thornycroft charabanc, possibly registration number CU 13, second hand from Musselburgh & District Tramways Co.

1911   Two charabancs, named "Pick me up" and "Pioneer". One of these may have been the 1910 Thornycroft.

1922   No 27 WY 4589; No 28 WY 4590; No 29 WY 4591. Daimler with Strachan and Brown front entrance, single deck bodies.

1925   No 30 WT 9876. Daimler with a Strachan and Brown front entrance single deck body.
No 32 WU 1234 and No 33 WU 1508. Dennis with Roe front entrance single deck bodies.

C 3420 "The Pioneer" decorated for King George V's coronation. Although the ownership panel reads "The Mexborough Motor Omnibus Co Ltd", it was certainly being operated by or on behalf of the Mexborough and Swinton Tramways Co. The conductor is in the tramway Company's uniform in every detail.
Courtesy P Tulley

1933   Nos 1 & 2 YG 2478-2479. Dennis with London Lorries front entrance single deck bodies.

1935   No 3 HE 3757. Second hand ex Yorkshire Traction Co. Leyland with Brush centre entrance single deck body.

1939   No 91 CP 6546. Second hand ex Hebble Motor Services. Albion with Eastern Coachworks front entrance single deck body.
Nos 385 and 386 HE 6008-6009 ex Yorkshire

Traction Co. Leyland with Roe front entrance single deck bodies.

1941   No 76 AWR 887 third hand from Yorkshire Traction Co. Originally with McAdoo. Albion with Barnsley Bodies rear entrance single deck body.
Two Leyland with Leyland bodies registered WF 829-830 were acquired from Sheffield United Tours. It is believed that they were never used by Mexborough & Swinton in passenger service.

No 43 (MWU 143), a Leyland with a Weymann 44 seat front entrance body which entered service in March 1954. There were ten buses in this batch. The design became the standard for the next six years and helped to cause the demise of the trolley buses.

Metamorphosis! No 49 (MWU 149) started life in 1954 painted the standard Mexborough green with service seating. During its life it was improved by fitting high back coach type seats and a cream livery for private party use etc. *Courtesy D Dodd*

No 57 (VWT 57) was new in 1960 - another Leyland - Weymann. It is followed by one of the new Leyland Atlanteans, No 5 (7005 WU), also with a Weymann body, when new in 1961. The buses are standing at the Rotherham terminus in Frederick Street, not long after the end of the Mexborough trolley buses.

1948   Nos 77-79 SWU 855-857. Bedford with Duple single deck front entrance bodies.

No 80 EBT 240 Third hand from East Yorkshire Motor Services. Originally with Crosby of Hunmanby. Bedford with Roe single deck front entrance body.

1949   Nos 81-82 HWV 479-480. Bedford with Duple single deck front entrance bodies.

1950   Nos 83-84 AWA 331-332. Second hand from Sheffield United Tours. Leyland with Duple single deck front entrance bodies.

1952   No 85 DDV 447; Nos 86-87 DDV 441-442; No 88 DDV 451. Second hand from Devon General. A.E.C. with Harrington front entrance single deck bodies.

No 9 (7009 WU) One of the Leyland Atlanteans with Weymann bodies which replaced the trolley buses on the Conisbrough - Rotherham route in 1961.

No 87 (DDV 442) an A.E.C. Regal with a Harrington front entrance body was purchased from Devon General in 1952. It was withdrawn next year and is seen here standing at the rear of Rawmarsh depot.

1954   Nos 40-49 MWU 140-149. Leyland with Weymann front entrance single deck bodies.

1955   Nos 100 OWU 660. Leyland with Burlingham single deck centre entrance coach body.
No 90 FKO 81 Second hand from Maidstone and District Motor Services. Leyland with E.C.W. single deck rear entrance body.

1957   Nos 50-51 SWW 50-51. Leyland with Weymann front entrance single deck "standee" bodies.

No 52 TWX 52 Leyland with Weymann front entrance single deck "standee" body.

1958   No 53 UWY 53. Leyland with Weymann front entrance single deck body.
No 101 UWY 101. Leyland with Burlingham single deck front entrance coach body.

1959   No 54 WWW 54. Leyland with Weymann single deck front entrance body.

1960   Nos 55-58 YWT 55-58. Leyland with Weymann single deck front entrance bodies.
Nos 1-11. 7001 WU - 7011 WU Leyland with Weymann double deck front entrance bodies.

A line up at Rawmarsh depot with No 90 (FKO 81) in use as a towing wagon, No 16 (FCD 511) as the centre piece with No 47 (MWU 147) as the only one of the three that was new to Mexborough and Swinton in 1954. *Courtesy A B Cross*

No 102 (XWX 376) a Ford Thames with a Plaxton body came to the Mexborough & Swinton in January 1961. It had belonged to Camplejohn Bros and passed to Yorkshire Traction who did not operate it but sold it on at once. It was photographed at Windsor - far from its normal territory. *Courtesy C Nash*

1961 No 12, 6812 WX. Leyland with Weymann double deck front entrance body.

No 102 XWX 376 Third hand from Yorkshire Traction Co. Originally with Camplejohn Bros. Ford with Plaxton single deck front entrance coach body.

Nos 15 and 16. FCD 509 and FCD 511. Second hand from Southdown Motor Services. Leyland with N.C.M.E. double deck rear entrance bodies.

1962 Nos 13 and 14, 8413 YC -8414 YC. Leyland with Weymann double deck front entrance bodies.

Nos 103, LCD 856 and 104-105 LCD 859 - LCD 860. Second hand from Southdown Motor Services. Leyland with Beadle single deck centre entrance coach bodies.

No 16 (FCD 511) Second hand from Southdown Motor Services in 1961. The Leyland TD5 chassis dated from January 1939 but the body in the illustration was built by N. C. M. E. in 1950.
Courtesy D Dodd

No 17 (JCD 29). Purchased from Southdown Motor Services in 1964. Dating from 1948 it was a Leyland PD2/1 with a Leyland body.

1963   Nos 15-18, registered GUF 667, 669, 671 and 682. Second hand from Southdown Motor services. Leyland with Park Royal double deck rear entrance bodies.

Nos 106-107 LUF 621 and 627. Ex Southdown Leyland with Leyland single deck centre entrance coach bodies.

1964   No 19 CWY 319B. Daimler with Weymann double deck front entrance body.

Nos 17 and 20. JCD 29 and JCD 39. Second hand from Southdown Motor Services. Leyland with Leyland double deck rear entrance bodies.

Nos 104-105. LUF 639 - LUF 640. Second hand from Southdown Motor Services. Leyland with Leyland single deck centre entrance coach bodies.

No 23 (KUF 722) started life as No 722 in the Southdown Motor Services fleet. A Leyland PD2/12 with a Leyland Body, it entered service in June 1951. It joined the Mexborough fleet in 1965 and was scrapped in 1968.
Courtesy D Dodd

No 113 (PIN 3) a Bedford SB5 with a Harrington body was new in 1963 when it joined the Northern General fleet. It came into the Mexborough & Swinton fleet in October 1967.
Courtesy M Fowler

1965 No 108 EWW 108 C. Leyland with Duple (Northern) single deck front entrance coach body.

Nos 21, 22, 23, 24, KUF 704, KUF 707, KUF 722, KUF 723 respectively. Second hand from Southdown Motor Services. Leyland with Leyland double deck rear entrance bodies.

No 103 OUF 834. Second hand from Southdown Motor Services. Leyland with Harrington single deck rear entrance coach body.

1966 No 109 KWW 109 D. Leyland with Duple (Northern) single deck front entrance coach body.

Mexborough and Swinto No 102-XWX. 376. To Mexborough & Swinton 1.1961. New to Camplejohn Brothers 6.59.
A Ford 570E - Plaxton C41F .To Mexborough and Swinton via Yorks Traction who did not operate it. Disposal July 1968.

1967 No 110. NWW 110 E. Leyland with Duple (Northern) single deck front entrance body.

Nos 15-18 and 20-21. RWV 515 F - RWV 518 F and RWV 520 F, RWV 521 F. Daimler with N.C.M.E. front entrance double deck bodies. Note Nos 15 to 18 were sold to West Riding Auto Co in March 1969.

Nos 112-114 PCN 2 - 4. Second hand from Northern General Transport Co. Bedford with Harrington single deck front entrance coach bodies.

1968 Nos 22-25, WWU 922 G - WWU 925 G. Daimler with N.C.M.E. double deck front entrance bodies.

No 115, 539 DWT. Second hand from Store (Reliance). Bedford with Yeates single deck front entrance "Dual purpose" body.

No 116, TDO 294. Second hand from Camplin and Sons. Bedford with Yeates single deck front entrance "dual purpose" body.

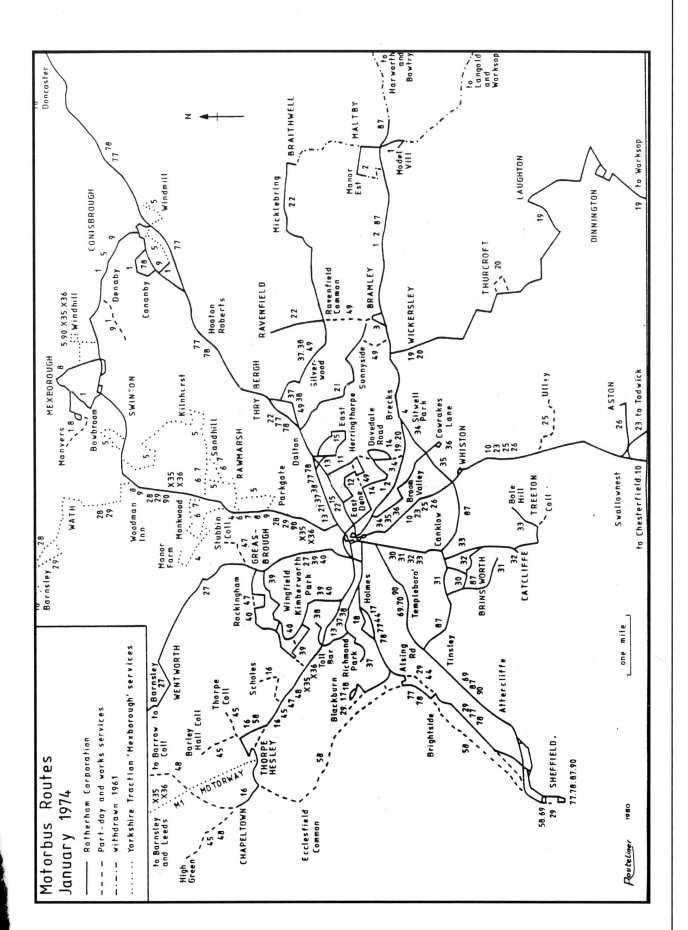

Motorbus Routes
January 1974

—————— Rotherham Corporation
– – – – Part-day and works services
– · – · – withdrawn 1961
············· Yorkshire Traction 'Mexborough' services

Routeliner 1980

one mile

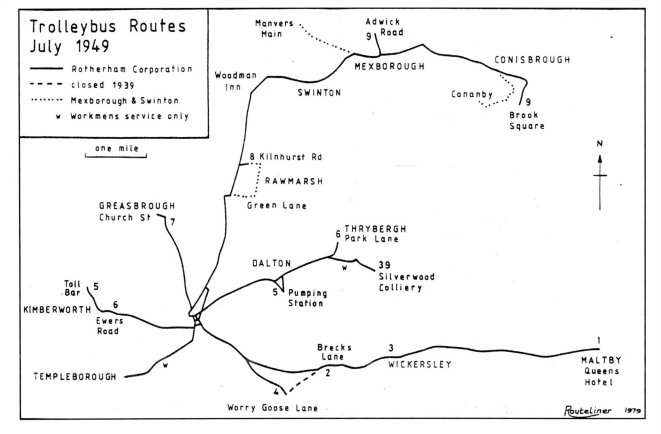

Trolleybus Routes July 1949

——— Rotherham Corporation
– – – closed 1939
········· Mexborough & Swinton
w Workmens service only

one mile

Manvers Main

Adwick Road
9

MEXBOROUGH

CONISBROUGH

Woodman Inn

SWINTON

Conanby

Brook Square
9

8 Kilnhurst Rd

RAWMARSH

Green Lane

GREASBROUGH Church St
7

THRYBERGH Park Lane
6

DALTON

39 Silverwood Colliery
w

5 Pumping Station

Toll Bar
5

KIMBERWORTH
6

Ewers Road

Brecks Lane

3

WICKERSLEY

1

MALTBY Queens Hotel

TEMPLEBOROUGH
w

2

4

Worry Goose Lane

N

Routeliner 1979